Growing Together As a Couple

Cornelia ~
all blessings on your
marriage! love -
Cheryl Brodersen

Growing Together As a Couple

BRIAN & CHERYL BRODERSEN

HARVEST HOUSE PUBLISHERS

EUGENE, OREGON

GROWING TOGETHER AS A COUPLE
Copyright © 2011 by Brian and Cheryl Brodersen
Published by Harvest House Publishers
Eugene, Oregon 97402
www.harvesthousepublishers.com

Library of Congress Cataloging-in-Publication Data
    Brodersen, Brian, 1956-
    Growing together as a couple / Brian and Cheryl Brodersen.
        p. cm.
    ISBN 978-0-7369-2794-9 (pbk.)
    ISBN 978-0-7369-4196-9 (eBook)
    1. Spouses—Religious life. 2. Marriage—Religious aspects—Christianity. I. Brodersen, Cheryl, 1960-
II. Title.
    BV4596.M3B76 2011
    248.8'44—dc23
                                                                2011031491

Printed in the United States of America

14 15 16 17 18 19 / BP-SK / 10 9 8 7 6 5 4 3 2

To the Lord Jesus Christ, the Great Shepherd of the sheep, who called us together as one. He has been faithful to work in us, love us, and be present with us in and through all things.

And to our children, who God in the richness of His grace blessed us with—our daughters, Kristyn and Kelsey, and our sons, Char and Braden. They have taught us many lessons, including the greatness of being able to laugh at ourselves. Oh what joy you all are to our hearts and lives!

Acknowledgments

We want to thank Harvest House for believing in this book and making it happen.

We also want to express our earnest appreciation to Hope Lyda for her hard and amazing work in transforming our offerings into something enjoyable. She has shown us grace a million times over.

Finally we would like to thank the rascals at the castle in Austria who videotaped our casual talk on marriage because they believed it would bless others. You know who you are!

Contents

Growing a Godly Marriage

Over and over in our marriage, we have seen how God is able to nurture and transform that which we have committed to Him. We've seen how God can take two hardheaded people and make them one in Christ. We've also witnessed how He can take two opposites and blend them together in such a unique way that they complement each other…to the point we can't even imagine not being together. We have seen how He brings together two people from different backgrounds, with different likes, dislikes, talents, and abilities, and fashions them so they are fruitful and blessed.

We want to celebrate and nurture the wonderful truth that marriage is a God thing—and therefore a good thing. According to the Bible, marriage originated out of God's desire for His children to have the very best human experience possible. In the first two chapters of Genesis we read,

> The Lord God said, "It is not good that man should be alone; I will make him a helper comparable to him"…And the Lord God caused a deep sleep to fall on Adam, and he slept; and He took one of his ribs, and closed up the flesh in its place. Then the rib that the Lord God had taken from the man He made into a woman, and He brought her to the man…Therefore a man shall leave his father and

mother and be joined to his wife, and they shall become one flesh…Then God saw everything that He had made, and indeed it was very good.

The declaration here is that marriage is good. It is God's gift to men and women for their mutual benefit and enjoyment. It's true! Marriage, if lived out according to His plan as revealed in the Scriptures, is one of the most blessed experiences possible in this life. That is what we have found over the past 30 years. And it's not because we're perfect (far from it); it's not because we've never struggled (we have); it's not because we always agree on everything (we don't); it's not because we never fight (we do). It is because, at the end of the day, we've decided to follow Christ and submit to His Word rather than follow the desires of our own hearts and live for ourselves.

The State of Marriage Today

A great apathy seems to have clouded the minds of the people of our nation when it comes to the importance of marriage. A record 70 percent of Americans believe divorce is morally acceptable, according to Gallup's 2008 Values and Belief survey. Two generations of high divorce rates have made divorce the norm in America. So much so that the U.S. has the highest divorce rate in the world. What was once regarded as a sacred union is now viewed by many as an arrangement worth trying when one is in love, but fine to dissolve for any number of reasons, from irreconcilable differences to an almost meaningless "we've grown apart."

As you and your spouse oppose this apathy and invest in growing together, it is important to be aware of all that can stand between you and your maturity in Christ. Open your eyes to these barriers and obstacles so you can fine-tune your efforts, your prayers, and your diligence as a faithful and faith-filled couple.

Three Ways to Miss the Essentials

There are all sorts of forces competing with and waging war against marriage. These forces almost always fall into one of three different categories—the world, the flesh, and the devil.

The influence of the *world* creeps into places you wouldn't expect. Many marriage manuals we have read, classes we've attended, or lectures we have heard on marriage provide us either with lists of stringent rules or with a few laughs rather than a greater understanding of how to make our marriage thrive.

One year Cheryl returned from a retreat visibly disturbed. When I asked her what was wrong, she related the following story. Some time ago, she had been talking to the wife of a couple we knew. The wife's husband had recently entered the ministry, and the wife was struggling regarding her husband as her pastor too. Before they had become Christians their marriage had suffered some severe blows and the husband had been unfaithful.

In vain, Cheryl had tried to encourage this young wife. Finally she suggested they attend a workshop on marriage together. The woman who taught the workshop began with a list of Victorian rules she had found in some nineteenth-century text. She then reiterated these rules as standards for today's marriages. One of those rules was that couples must rise at the same time in the morning and go to bed at the same time at night.

As Cheryl listened, she realized that our marriage was being disqualified as righteous or godly. The teacher left no room for grace or individuality. And my wife returned home from that event with a bit of a broken heart and a list of what was wrong with our marriage, according to the speaker.

But do you know what? Nothing was wrong with our marriage. Not one of the rules presented had any biblical basis. Though the woman that gave the lecture was well-meaning, she was off track. I don't think Cheryl was the only wife who left that workshop discouraged.

We receive unbiblical advice from many places. The "world" enters our homes and marriages through input we receive from sources not grounded in godly wisdom, including some strangers and some friends, media portals, and people of influence who don't measure their words against God's Word but who have huge platforms from which to address mass audiences and impact how people think and live. If we gather our thoughts and principles about marriage from these worldly sources, we're going to end up with some pretty bad advice, mixed information, and a whole lot of confusion.

Cheryl receives a magazine that has great crossword puzzles. Every week this same magazine features both a diet *and* recipes for fattening desserts. In the same way, the world tries to give license to destructive practices while still claiming to have the best solutions for failing relationships.

The *flesh*, which is our own desire and selfishness, is another force that wages war against marriage. Our self-focused desires left unchecked will wreak havoc on our spouse and our marriage. Selfishness can never be fully appeased. Feed it, and it will only grow more wanton until it eats away everything.

Finally, every married couple has God's archenemy as their personal foe. The *devil* wants to destroy marriage because it is God's institution to protect and promote the well-being, joy, and health of His creation. We will delve more fully into Satan's wiles against marriage in Essential Seven—enlightenment. Until then suffice it to say that the devil is a formidable foe.

In order for a marriage to survive today, let alone thrive, believers need to be equipped with clear biblical principles that they can allow God to work out individually in their marriage. In the ten essentials that follow this introduction, we have done our best to distill the message of the Scriptures for you in a practical, memorable way. And you'll hear a lot from Cheryl and me about how these essentials have shaped, corrected, and guarded our own relationship. (Believe me, there's a lot to tell!)

Growing Pains

Cheryl and I are two strong-willed passionate people who got married after knowing each other for a whole five months! We realized very quickly that we didn't know each other very well at all. Our differences were significant. I loved surfing and wanted to hit the waves as often as I could. She loved the idea of being married to a surfer, as long as he surfed only when it was beach weather. I wanted to listen to music on the radio while we drove in the car. Cheryl loved music but preferred to talk while we traveled. I loved staying up till all hours of the night reading and talking; she fell asleep once the sun set.

We discovered what all couples discover: We are two very different people, now married for better or for worse. Unfortunately, our relationship was leaning toward the "worse" option rather than the "better" goal. We fought about one thing or another every single day of our first year of marriage, and probably every other day of our second year.

Our bickering drew the attention of a pastor friend of mine, who advised me that our marriage probably wouldn't last at the rate we were going. After all, we were not fitting into the mold of what a Christian couple was supposed to look like. Despite the less-than-encouraging comment, I knew that Cheryl and I loved each other; we felt that God had brought us together, and divorce was not an option. I had come from a broken home, and the last thing I wanted was a repeat of what I had lived through as a child. So, we removed the word *divorce* from our vocabulary and simply hung in there. It wasn't long before the fights began to diminish in length, passion, and frequency. They were replaced with an enduring love, a great friendship, godly encouragement, and mutual enjoyment.

Two individuals can become united in heart and direction when God is their foundation, center, and focus. This is when a marriage truly grows.

What It Takes to Grow Together

Because we paid attention to the condition of our marriage and sought out God's help and strength for our union, our marriage has grown in God's direction. People notice and remark how much Cheryl and I enjoy each other's company after our 30 years of marriage. And we truly do. We now have more in common and fewer differences than ever. We even find ourselves, at times, thinking the same thought. At least there are times I know what she is thinking and vice-versa.

About ten years ago, while we were living in England, Cheryl was asked to do a workshop on marriage. As she pondered what she would say, the Lord impressed on her the idea of seven essentials for a blessed marriage. She wrote them down and got some of my comments on each point. She then prepared a lecture, praying that God would guide her and wanting to be as transparent and Spirit-led as possible. After she spoke, the women at the retreat were so inspired by the message she shared that they asked her if they could transcribe it and put it in a booklet for their next retreat. Cheryl agreed, and that transcription is the basis for what we are doing in this book.

Last year, we presented those same ideas rather spontaneously to gatherings in both England and Austria. With only our list of the essentials in front of us, we shared with those congregated. The response was incredible. We were amazed to see how these simple instructions helped and encouraged so many couples.

A friend of ours sat behind a couple who had come to us earlier in the week struggling with their relationship. Our friend noticed that the couple seemed to warm to each other as we were sharing. First they began to smile at each other as they related to the issues we had dealt with. Soon they were laughing. After a time the woman put her hand through her husband's arm and leaned her head on his shoulder. They left the conference with a renewed commitment to their marriage and a fresh sense of love for one another.

As we write this book together, Cheryl and I will share different thoughts, attitudes, and stories just as we did when we were in Europe. It is our prayer that God would use these ten essentials to help you embrace a deeper, clearer understanding and appreciation of what God has given to you and ordained for you through your marriage.

To help you distinguish the points where one or the other of us comes in individually, we have given monograms to each of our sections. They will start like this:

B = Brian   **C** = Cheryl

Our intention is for husbands and wives to glean from both of our offerings. However, there are a few selections written directly to men and directly to women. These will be set apart with a different design and the headings "A Word to the Men" and "A Word to the Women."

Cheryl and I together will open chapters and welcome you to each growing-together essential, and we'll close together to lead you into the "Knowing Is Growing" questions and ideas for discussion and the "Growing-Together Grace" prayers.

The Reward of Marriage

As we enter our fourth decade of marriage we look forward to all that God has planned for the days ahead. It feels a bit like we are entering the harvesting stage of the seeds we've sown over the past 30 years. Our kids are all grown now and we are seeing the blessed fruit of having sown into their lives. We're watching them get married; we're seeing them have children; we're observing them serve the Lord, live by faith, and bear fruit for the kingdom; and we are getting to enjoy it together.

The world's diversions and versions of life cannot compare to living the way God intended for us to live. His ways are fulfilling, exciting, and enjoyable. The world offers a cheap substitute that will leave you empty, unhappy, and aimless. God's plan—one man, one woman, for life—is the way to go, and the dividends are an abundance of love, joy, peace, security, happiness, and…a whole lot of fun!

KNOWING IS GROWING

1. Discuss times when you've received or read poor advice for your marriage. What aspects of that advice, in light of God's love and His Word, can you let go of right here and now?

2. How have you felt the world, flesh, and the devil pressing you toward negative views on marriage or on your marriage?

3. Why are you excited to grow together as a couple? Why is it important to you, your family, and to God? Talk about why this is the right moment to be investing time, communication, prayer, and faith in your marriage.

GROWING-TOGETHER GRACE

Lord, You are the Creator of marriage and the maker of our hearts. We gratefully acknowledge that the seeds of truth and hope we plant today will become a longtime harvest of joy and faith for us and for our family. Release us from the bondage of bad advice and deceptive interpretations of Your best for us. Walk with us in this journey, Lord. Please bless our marriage and give us the strength and faithfulness to take each step closer to one another and to Your heart.

Essential
ONE:

Entrust

A Prayer for My Spouse

May _____ be "filled with the knowledge of His will in all wisdom and spiritual understanding" and "walk worthy of the Lord, fully pleasing Him, fruitful in every good work and increasing in the knowledge of God." May (he or she) be "strengthened with all might, according to His glorious power, for all patience and longsuffering with joy."

FROM COLOSSIANS 1:9-11

Entrust

For those who have been single for a while or who have strong personalities, it isn't easy to realize that decisions, needs, dreams, responsibilities, finances, faith, commitments, and every other part of life are about the *two* of you. It takes concerted effort and awareness to avoid power plays and unhealthy expectations that can set a relationship up for failure or at least unhappiness. The seed of conflict is planted in a marriage when husbands and wives try to change or control one another.

The secret to a happy union isn't for your spouse to wake up one day and suddenly have exactly the same concerns and priorities as you. The key to letting go of unreal expectations is to seek God's strength and covering. Learning to entrust the security of your marriage and spouse to the Lord is the best lesson anyone can learn for all areas of life.

In this chapter, we'll explore a very essential essential: Entrusting your spouse, marriage, family, actions, job, hopes, dreams, and worries to the Lord. This will lead you to a wonderful state of dependence on God and His very best for your marriage and life. An instrumental way to release a sense of control and expectation is to pray for each other daily. We often learn the hard way that in some instances, most instances, it is far better to talk to *God* about an issue we have with our spouse before we talk directly to our spouse.

Let's look at practical ways to entrust your life and marriage to God.

Giving to God What Matters Most

B Over the years, I've traveled a fair amount for the ministry. When I was gone for weeks at a time, I had to learn to entrust my wife and family to the Lord. This wasn't easy. I'm someone who checks and double-checks to make sure doors, windows, screens, and other openings around the house are locked up securely. This habit—and the concern behind it—may have developed because when I was younger my home was robbed several times. But I believe that most every man wants to feel assured that his family is safe and sound.

Once, before I'd fully embraced this particular marriage essential, I returned from a trip and asked the kids how Mom had managed the security measures in my absence. And of course, they shared tales that ignited my worst fears: doors unlocked, windows wide open at all hours, and the garage door left up all night. If it hadn't been clear before, it was clear now: Cheryl was never going to be as security-focused as I wanted her to be. She was not going to carry that sense of worry I did. It was time for me to let go of that expectation. But that is no small thing. Have you tried to let go of an expectation you've placed on your spouse?

What Is Entrustment?

When Cheryl and I got married, we discovered our differences. And with each of those discoveries, we likely set some of our expectations of each other. For example, I was always ready to accept any invitation to socialize. Cheryl was much more likely to opt for a quiet evening at home. This led to many heated exchanges because I wanted to persuade Cheryl that she needed to be more social. And I'm sure she was hoping that I'd realize how nice it was to cozy up, just the two of us, each evening.

I finally gave up trying to convince her to be more like me and just accepted that we were different. When we understand one another and seek to know each other fully, it becomes a chance to discover what our spouse uniquely brings to our relationship. This is a big leap in spiritual and marital maturity. And it can take time.

My prayers eventually reflected this shift of acceptance and understanding. When I lifted up prayers for Cheryl, I prayed that God would make her into the person He wanted her to be, not the one I wanted her to be. Then, much to my amazement, she ultimately became every bit, if not more, a people person like me. And it wasn't to please me or appease me. Her changes were part of God's path of growth for her. The impact on her life, our ministry, and our marriage was significant. We still marvel at that change today.

Conforming or Entrusting?

Many of us try to conform our spouses into our image because we forget that they are made in God's image and are destined to be conformed to the image of Christ. We forget that we are made and intended to complement rather than duplicate one another. If we were identical, we wouldn't grow much. God brings opposites together, or two unique individuals together, so we can both grow into a more complete person than we'd be on our own.

I am a new and improved version of me as a result of being married to Cheryl. She has taught me how to love and care for others; how to give of myself so others will be blessed. Yet in the early days I would have unintentionally circumvented all that by insisting she be more like me rather than entrusting her to God so she could become the person He wanted her to be.

Sooner or later, every married person will have to learn to entrust their spouse to God if they want to enjoy marriage as He intended. When this happens sooner, you will reap the rewards of a closer relationship for many years.

What area of life do you need to give over to God's care? What do you need to entrust to His capable hands and His perfect wisdom?

Entrusting Your Spouse to God

What does entrusting our spouse to God look like on a practical, doable level? Men need to remember that women are sometimes more sensitive about certain topics or concerns than we are. On numerous occasions I've attempted to help Cheryl with something that I thought needed addressing, only to send us into World War III. I'll never forget the time she asked me if I thought it would be a good idea to put our children in school. She had homeschooled them during the three-and-a-half years we lived in England and continued to do so for about a year after we returned home to the States. Before she posed the question, I also had been thinking that it might be a good idea to enter the kids into the school system now that we were settled in the U.S. again. So my response was in favor. As I went on about why the change was a good plan, I said that I thought they would get a better education. Can you guess what happened next?

The moment those words fell from my lips, I knew I had made a big mistake. But foolishly, I didn't stop there. I proceeded to explain what I'd really meant, but to no avail. Cheryl interpreted my comment to mean that she was a failure as a teacher and unfit to be a mother. Of course, I hadn't said anything like that! But sometimes, wives have this amazing way of hearing things we've never said or even thought to say. Like the time Cheryl asked me how I liked the meal she had prepared and I responded with "It's fine," which to her meant, "You're a terrible cook and I wish I had a different wife!"

I'm still learning to apply that great bit of wisdom from the epistle of James, "Let every man be swift to hear, slow to speak…" Listening and praying, that's what entrusting looks like on a practical level.

And the praying is specific. I like to pray for Cheryl to excel in every area of her life. She's first and foremost a Christian, so I pray that God will give to her the Spirit of wisdom and revelation in the knowledge of Himself, that He would fulfill all His good pleasure in and through her life. She's also a mother, so I pray for her relationship with our children. She's my wife, and there are things that pertain specifically to our relationship as husband and wife that I pray about. As a Christian, she's a servant of Jesus Christ, and I want her to enter into all that God has called her to.

I didn't always think like this. Early on in my work as a pastor I looked at her involvement with the women's ministry at the church as an inconvenience. It seemed to take so much time away from the family. Sometimes I was stuck with the kids for hours, and on a few occasions I even had to make them dinner! Can you imagine a man having to look out for his own kids for a few hours a week? Unthinkable! Well, that just shows you how clueless I've been at times in this marriage.

I've since realized that not only does God have a call on my life in regard to the ministry of His Word, He also has a call on Cheryl's life—and I want to do all I can to assist her. Praying for her is a great way of doing that.

Have you been able to give your spouse over to the Lord? If yes, how have you grown closer to each other? If not, then consider what areas of your husband's or wife's life you are resistant to release to God's care. Ask yourself, and God, why these particular aspects of your loved one are difficult to surrender. It's not surprising that the tough-to-let-go areas of our spouse's life are the areas we most want to control! Pray for discernment so you can honor your marriage and your spouse.

One of the greatest blessings of the marriage relationship is what Peter refers to as "being heirs together of the grace of life." That's what we are, and the best way to assure the fullness of God's blessing on your marriage is to pray for it.

Nurture Instead of Nag

C I have to admit that, in the same way Brian wanted to "conform" me to his image, I wanted to "fix" him. I married a darling young surfer with tons of potential...all he needed was a little fixing up.

When I met Brian he had a furnished apartment and some pretty cool clothes. However, when we arrived at our first apartment together I was aghast to find that he had reduced all his belongings to fit into two paper bags. One bag held past issues of a sports magazine and a trophy that a runner from Denmark had given him. The other bag held all his clothes, toiletries, and possessions. It was easy to see this guy needed some help!

I think many women are naturally drawn to fixer-uppers. We are nurturers. We want to add our touch and our improvements to houses, gardens, and the like—which unfortunately often carries over to our husbands. After all, when we married them we knew we could greatly improve them!

I discovered that Brian was not receptive to my helpful suggestions. When he didn't listen to me, I found myself scheming, screaming, and doing just about anything I could to convince him of the need of change. I tried in vain to help him break bad habits, improve his manners, and look his best.

Rather than helping, I was trying to control Brian. That's what it felt like to him and that's what it looked like to others. My suggestions quickly deteriorated into nagging. Now, who wants to be around a nagging woman? Proverbs 21:19 states, "Better to dwell in the wilderness, than with a contentious and angry woman." I think Brian must have shared the sentiments of Solomon (the author of Proverbs)!

My nature had become so contrary that my husband could no longer hear me on any issue. We came to many impasses in our marriage, points where any helpful suggestion I made was refused. He wouldn't even listen to me. And I couldn't move him in any way.

In utter desperation, I began to pray. At first, I prayed for Brian to change. And he did. He began to listen to me. When he wouldn't budge, I took it to God. God would speak to Brian, and Brian would yield to God. It was amazing.

I was slowly being transformed from the contentious wife to the praying wife.

After a time, my prayers begin to change in their nature. No longer was I praying for a change in Brian, but I was praying for blessing, spiritual revelation, wisdom, and godly authority. I was praying he would be a good father to our kids and a godly role model. I begin to take scriptures and pray them for Brian.

One of my favorite passages to pray is Colossians 1:9-11—that my husband would be "filled with the knowledge of His will in all wisdom and spiritual understanding"; that he would "walk worthy of the Lord, fully pleasing Him, fruitful in every good work and increasing in the knowledge of God"; that he would be "strengthened with all might, according to His glorious power, for all patience and longsuffering with joy."

Brian has chronic fatigue syndrome, so I also began to pray for his health and stamina. I prayed that faith would raise him up on the days when his strength failed. I prayed Isaiah 40:31 over him, that he would wait on the Lord and that his strength would be renewed. I prayed he would mount up on wings as an eagle, that he would run and not be weary, and be empowered to walk and not faint.

How Prayer Changes a Marriage

Do you know what happened as I prayed? *I* changed. My desires for Brian changed. I took on God's perspective about him. You see, God loves my husband. God, Himself, called my husband. God saved my husband and delivered him from sin, death, and aimlessness. God placed my husband in the ministry and made him a shepherd over his flocks. God gifted my husband to teach and serve the church. I received, through prayer, a new respect, appreciation, and love for him. I no longer wanted to fix him up (except on occasions—no one's perfect), but enjoy him.

Every day I pray for Brian. Every day God and I meet to talk about my husband's needs. A year ago, Brian and I were walking on the beach. He kept complaining about a certain situation. I knew there was nothing we could do about it and told him so. However, he didn't want to let it go. The more he talked, the more incensed and depressed he got. None of my godly encouragements were hitting the mark. In fact, everything I said seemed to be fuel for the fire of discontentment in his heart. I knew he needed prayer, but I was getting discouraged. I told him I wouldn't walk with him if he mentioned that subject anymore. (No, I am not always nice.) When he broached it again, I took off walking in a different direction toward home. He was forced to walk back to our car.

My walk home was long. With each step, I prayed for Brian. "Lord, he needs You so desperately right now. He needs an Emmaus road experience with You."

Emmaus road was the route two of the disciples of Jesus walked a few days after the crucifixion. Dejected and downcast, they discussed the death of Jesus and rumors of His resurrection. As they walked and talked, a stranger drew near and spoke with them. He expounded the Scriptures to them and explained why it was necessary for the Messiah to suffer, die, and rise again from the dead. As the man spoke, the men's hearts burned within them. They asked him to join them for supper.

As the stranger gave thanks and broke the bread in their presence, they suddenly realized that He was Jesus! At the very moment they recognized Him, Jesus disappeared before them. Filled with absolute elation they ran back to Jerusalem to tell the other disciples they had seen the risen Lord and what He had spoken to them. The disciples in their grief and depression had not realized the glory that the risen Jesus was actually walking and talking with them.

Yes. Brian needed that same experience. He couldn't understand the difficulties he was facing. He needed to be alone with Jesus and have Jesus speak to him. That was my prayer.

We both arrived home at the same time. Brian climbed out of the car with a huge smile. "Jesus met me," he said. I knew He had. Not only was Brian's countenance changed, but I had also felt the sweet assurance of God's Spirit as I walked.

It was a different conversation between the two of us that evening as we talked about the power of our risen Lord—much, I imagine, as those disciples had done 2000 years before.

God knows what your husband needs. And He longs to meet your husband where he's at in a struggle, a decision, a trial, or a success. So, entrust him to God in prayer. When he won't hear you—pray. When he is struggling—pray. When he is confused—pray. When he is pursuing truth—pray. When he is tempted—pray. When he is embracing God's purpose in his life—pray. Pray...pray...pray!

Bless This Marriage, Lord

I read the journal of a woman who lived at the turn of the twentieth century. On the pages she was bemoaning the struggles in her marriage.

Her critical mother-in-law had moved in with them. Her husband was gone for long hours at his job and didn't understand the hardship of sharing the house with a contrary person. The wife's attempts to communicate her despair to her spouse were met with accusations of complaining.

At this desperate point, she prays for her marriage. And what is interesting is this—she adds a request for God to bless her marriage. She starts to add this request to every prayer. Soon she found her husband was doing the same. After some time they were praying together for God to bless their marriage. The journal ended with the woman attributing the blessed estate of their long and happy marriage to the prayers they prayed for it.

As I read this journal, I was taken with the thought of praying for my marriage and was surprised I had never thought to do so. I guess I had simply assumed that since Brian and I were both Christians and both called to the ministry we would naturally be blessed.

It was about that time that my personal Bible reading fell upon John 2, the wedding at Cana of Galilee. The Scripture states, "Jesus and His disciples were invited to the wedding" (verse 2). Jesus was at the wedding because He was invited. During His time there must have been thousands of marriages between righteous men and women that He did not attend. But He attended this one because He was invited to it.

Not only did Jesus attend this wedding, but also He blessed it. It wasn't long into the celebration when the wine ran out. This could have been disastrous to the couple and deemed a bad omen by those who came to the wedding. Mary, Jesus' mother, knowing the seriousness of the issue, went to Jesus. When she told her son the problem, in true rabbinic manner He answered her with a question. (The rabbis of Jesus' time would often ask their disciples questions in return to draw out from them the motivation or understanding behind the disciples' original questions.) At this occasion, Jesus asked His mother, "What does your concern have to do with Me?" Jesus wanted her to recognize the natural correlation she made between need and Jesus.

Only Jesus could meet the need at the wedding.

He ordered the servants to fill up six purified earthen vessels with water. The servants enthusiastically filled these plain pots to the brim and brought them back. Jesus then ordered them to take some of the contents and present it as wine to the master of the feast. The servants did as they were commanded, and the result was amazing. The master of the feast declared the wine that Jesus had made to be superior to the wine that he had drunk at the beginning of the feast.

In the same manner, inviting Jesus into your marriage and asking Him for His blessing is a guarantee that every deficiency, whether emotional, financial, spiritual, or physical, will be met by His sufficiency.

Years ago, just like the woman whose journal I mentioned, I started putting a little addendum to my prayers—"Lord, bless my marriage." When I prayed with Brian, I would add, "Lord, bless our marriage." It wasn't long before he started adding the same ending to his prayers.

As Brian loves to say, "Marriage is God's thing." God created marriage for His divine purposes. God brought Eve to Adam and then walked with them every day in the cool of the afternoon before sin spoiled their fellowship. By prayer and entrustment that opportunity to walk together with God every day is restored.

So when we entrust our marriage to God we are asking Him to make Himself known in it and use it for His glorious purposes. We are even more committed to our marriage because it belongs to Him, and we belong to Him.

Entrusting Your Marriage to Jesus

We have found that ever since we started asking God to bless our marriage, He has in amazing and unexpected ways. We can both honestly say that we are more in love now than when we first said our vows. Our times together are enlightening, entertaining, and downright enjoyable. We have wondrous fellowship together too.

Our kids have also noted the state of our marriage and feel the security of parents who are united in heart and spirit, and in the Lord. Our two oldest children have both married wonderful soul mates, for which we thank Jesus every day.

Friends, Jesus wants you to trust Him to bless your marriage even as He blessed the wedding in Cana. Jesus wants to walk with you and your spouse on a daily basis. Start praying for His blessing upon your marriage. Start praying for your spouse and watch God begin to transform everything—your heart, their heart, your relationship, your family, your dreams, your purpose, and your future.

KNOWING IS GROWING

1. What about your partner do you need to entrust to God? Discuss these areas with one another and then pray about them. Your spouse might shed some light on areas they think you have a hard time giving to God. Hear what your loved one is saying so you can grow in this important essential.

2. Which personal insufficiencies should you be giving over to the absolute sufficiency of Christ? Think of one or two practical ways for you to give these needs over to God this week. For example, if you struggle with anger you might decide to 1) write out a prayer to name the area of insufficiency so you can give it to God, and 2) avoid or limit situations you know give rise to your anger.

3. Have you had a road-to-Emmaus experience (Luke 24:13-35)? What was it like, and how did it change you or your understanding of Jesus? What about that special encounter can encourage you in your faith and marriage today?

4. How has being married positively shaped your faith and life so far? Share these positive praises with one another.

GROWING-TOGETHER GRACE

Dear Lord, help us entrust one another to Your care. Thank You for the gift of marriage. As we seek Your Word and guidance, direct us to nurture each other with kind words, godly wisdom, and tenderness. Let us come to You daily with prayers for ourselves, our spouse, and our union. Help each of us release any desire to control or change the other so we can celebrate our differences and honor Your work in our spouse's life and in our own. Bless our marriage, Lord. We entrust it to You. Amen.

Essential
TWO:
Eliminate

Put on the Lord Jesus Christ, and make no provision for the flesh, to fulfill its lusts.

Romans 13:14

Eliminate

I f you're allergic to anything, you likely do everything you can to avoid an encounter with your particular problem food or other allergen. We have a niece who is so sensitive to peanuts that just being in their vicinity can trigger a life-threatening reaction. Whatever a person's allergen is, whether it is a cat, a food, or a particular plant, they will do all they can to eliminate or avoid those triggers.

What's this have to do with marriage? you ask. Well, we can guarantee that there are some allergens that are toxic to your marriage and your spiritual well-being.

There are certain things that, if allowed a permanent place in our marriages, can have far-reaching negative and even destructive effects. What do we do? The same as anyone whose well-being is threatened by a contaminate: We must eliminate, get rid of, put an end to, do away with, terminate, eradicate, annihilate, stamp out, wipe out, and throw out anything that is working against our husband-and-wife relationship becoming all that God intends it to be.

The patriarch Jacob was called by God to return to Bethel, the place where he had first met the Lord. He was given the promise of blessing if he returned so God could reaffirm His covenant with him. When Jacob heard God's call to return to Bethel he gathered his family together and said to them, "Put away the foreign gods that are among you, purify yourselves" (Genesis 35:1-15).

Jacob understood that if he and his family were to experience the full blessing that God intended for them, certain things would need to be eliminated. What were those things? The foreign gods. The idols!

Putting Away Childish Things

It is amazing how easy it is for men to make an idol out of something. No, we don't mean a statue to a foreign god. We mean the idols that we create in our culture or by our own preferences or obsessions. An idol is that thing you're most passionate about. Sports: playing sports, watching sports, talking sports. Money: making money, spending money, talking money, hoarding money. Objects: cars, boats, houses, surfboards, golf clubs, guitars, technology, computer games, clothing, food, and so on. You name it and it's almost certain that someone has made an idol of it. The list for each person is as unique as they are. And when you combine a man and woman in marriage, you get quite an assortment of possible idols that will take priority in that relationship.

All the activities and items we listed are pretty harmless on their own, and in some cases, even good in and of themselves. However, if we lose the proper perspective on them, we give them more importance in our lives than we should, and we become idol-worshipers who are threatening our own spiritual and marital well-being.

Idols and Idle Pursuits

B I know firsthand about struggling with idolatry. From the time I caught my first wave at age 13, I was hooked on surfing. Between the ages of 16 and 20, I rarely missed a day of gliding over the water.

Then when I married Cheryl, as I mentioned in the introduction, I naively thought she would love to sit on the beach all day and watch me surf. Every day off, guess where we would go? That's right—to the beach so I could surf, and so she could watch and admire.

Or so I thought.

As tensions welled up between us, I knew we had a problem. Yet I was stubborn and quite determined to keep up with my surfing. We spent years contending with each other over this issue. I tried to justify my actions by labeling this all-consuming interest as a proper, if not very healthy, habit.

In hindsight, I can see how unbelievably selfish I was. But it took awhile for me to wake up. I recall times when I should've been at home or out for a fun day with Cheryl and the kids—but instead, there I was out in the surf, waiting for that one last great wave that never seemed to come.

I was miserable much of the time because I was under the conviction of the Holy Spirit. And slowly but surely, I began to see that my priorities were totally out of whack. I started making the changes the Lord had been pressing me toward, and I started listening to my wife's perfectly reasonable request that I start acting like a man, a husband, and a father, and stop acting like a teenager. To put it simply, I began to put childish things aside.

It's not as though I've never struggled with those issues again—I've got similar stories about golf (the game I swore I'd never play) and a few other childish obsessions. Yet the Lord showed me that He intended for my relationship with my wife and kids to flourish and not falter. He showed me I needed to eliminate my childish behavior if I was going to ever be a healthy, whole, and godly man.

A WORD TO THE MEN:

Eliminating Fantasy and Temptations

B Fantasies are dangerous. Indulging in them is a setup for frustration, discontent, and failure. Some men mentally hold on to previous relationships so they can fantasize about what could have been. They compare their wife to other women they have known or have had relationships with.

To stay strongly rooted in your life and marriage and your walk with Christ, you must eliminate close relations with anyone you've had sexual or romantic feelings toward. There is no place in a marriage for a third party. Ever.

Some men tell me that they think it is okay to maintain close relationships with former girlfriends or ex-wives, even when their wives have objected to it. These men often say it's fine to go out for a cup of coffee with an old girlfriend. They'll come up with a dozen reasons why it is completely healthy to communicate by phone, e-mail, or text message with an old flame—which happens to be a really appropriate way to say it! Solomon asked the rhetorical question, "Can a man take fire to his chest and not be burned?" The answer is obviously no!

Most cases of infidelity in marriage start off rather innocently. There's an emotional attachment before there's a sexual encounter. Men, let me say it again: Eliminate close relationships with members of the opposite sex. They are inappropriate for a Christian man and ultimately detrimental to your marriage.

Letting go of past attachments is a way to rid your present of the toxicity of fantasies.

Putting the Past Behind

Relationships with women are not the only part of a man's past that he tends to cling to. Many men resist or lament growing up and becoming responsible. There's something in our nature and in our culture that encourages us to try to hold on to our youth forever, even at the cost of our personal growth and well-being. Look at all the aging rockers who just refuse to accept the fact that they are old men. It's sad to see, and even sadder to listen to them!

We're even being told today not to worry because 50 is the new 40 and 40 is the new 30. Americans, especially we Californians, want to stay young forever. But God wants us to grow up. He's calling you and me to put away childish attitudes and be responsible husbands and fathers. And He wants women to be responsible wives and mothers. Holy, healthy marriages are formed when men and women eliminate those things that are competing with their marriages for attention, care, and energy.

Are you married but still living like you're single? Out with the guys in the evenings? Out with the boys for the weekend to pursue hobbies that have now become toxic to your marriage? The Bible says that a man shall leave his father and mother and cleave to his wife. It could just as easily say, a man shall leave his childhood buddies and cleave to his wife!

I'm not recommending that you quit spending time with good friends occasionally any more than I'd suggest that once you leave your father and mother, you should have no further association with them. It's a matter of placing the correct importance on each relationship. Your wife and family are now your God-appointed priorities. Celebrate this gift and this privilege.

Eliminate Sexual Temptations and Sins

I'll be candid about this important topic: Sexual immorality is the main cause, from the male standpoint, of marital failure today. Men are out of control sexually! Pornography is rampant in the culture and astoundingly prevalent in the church. We cannot think we are immune to temptation. In fact, that kind of expectation is exactly what gets Christian men into trouble. If a man does indulge in pornography or fantasizing, he thinks he is the only one facing this struggle. The secret grows into greater sins and greater guilt. We aren't immune. And each man should know that the struggle is real, it's there, and it can be eliminated with God's help.

Most every man who grew up during or after the sexual revolution of the 1960s and 1970s wages a daily battle with overexposure to and overfascination with sex. I was looking at *Playboy* and *Penthouse* magazines as an adolescent, and by my mid-teens my life was pretty much dominated by fulfilling my sexual desires. During my high-school years, friends and

I would compete to see how many girls we could sleep with. Our view of sexuality was so distorted that we considered this perfectly normal and acceptable behavior. My dad was proud that his son would bring home a different girl every weekend!

I'm not being blunt for shock value. To say less than the truth about my past is to diminish the enormity of this issue for me and countless other men. Candy-coating the facts or talking around this topic rather than speaking right to the heart of it is a disservice to your personal and spiritual well-being. This is the real world as I, and virtually everyone I knew, experienced it. And all this was before the advent of the Internet. It's only gotten worse since.

Sexual obsession is a daily battle because Satan bombards us with memories and images from our past to try to ensnare us once again. We cannot give him any ground whatsoever. The enemy will never be satisfied until we are completely destroyed. His aim is to destroy not only our marriages, but our lives and our children's lives. Don't give him the satisfaction of being untrue to your purity and to the sanctity of your marriage.

Ridding Your Life of Pornography

Pornography can be found anywhere you choose to seek it: on the Internet, on cable channels, in a stash of magazines, or in the wilds of your imagination. If pornography has become a part of your life to any degree and in any form, it must be eradicated. If you have to disconnect your Internet and cable service because of a lack of self-control, then do it! If you have to avoid stopping at places that sell pornographic or sexually charged materials, then do it!

Some years ago we were visiting some friends in Spain. In that country the women like to sunbathe without their clothes on. It didn't take me long to realize that if I was going to spend time at the beach, it would have to be early morning before the sunbathers came out, or later after they'd gone back to their hotels. I've occasionally had a man tell me that he's not affected by the sight of scantily clad women, and so he doesn't need to worry about what he sees and is free to browse the Internet. He claims he can look over the latest swimsuit edition of *Sports Illustrated* or the Victoria's Secret catalog and even view anything he likes on cable. All I can say about a man like that is he's under a strong delusion and is already in the grip of the enemy.

Where are you in this struggle? Do you keep porn far away from you, or is it something you're immersed in and can't find your way out of? There really isn't an in-between state. Men try to justify "just looking" as a safe place that doesn't impact their thought lives or their marriages. But that is pure deception talking.

Victory over every form of sexual immorality is attainable. By the grace of God and the power of the Holy Spirit, we can be free from the bondage of sexual sin and safeguard our marriages from that destructive element. But how?

1. Consider how sexual immorality greatly offends God and ultimately brings about His judgment unless we repent. As Paul said,

> No fornicator, unclean person, nor covetous man, who is an idolater, has any inheritance in the kingdom of Christ and God. Let no one deceive you with empty words, for because of these things the wrath of God comes upon the sons of disobedience. Therefore do not be partakers with them. For you were once darkness, but now you are light in the Lord (Ephesians 5:5-8).

As I alluded to earlier, I came to Christ out of a sexually immoral lifestyle and understood from the very start of my spiritual commitment that my sexually impure behavior was unacceptable to God. I still know this to be true today. I don't want to do anything that would grieve the Spirit of God. I realize and respect my utter dependence upon Him to do what I do, and I would never want to risk grieving or quenching Him or jeopardizing the calling that He's placed on my life. I also do not want to disgrace the name of Christ and cause the many people who have entrusted themselves to me as their pastor to stumble, to doubt, to fall. I shudder at the thought.

Whether you are a minister, corporate lawyer, plumber, counselor, or bank teller, you are a child of God who has been called to a purpose and a path. Pornography is a deceptive path that leads only to the destruction of your faithful attention to God's call. What do you risk each time you consider viewing a website that sexually exploits women? What are you risking when you let your thoughts spiral into fantasy? Consider not only your losses, but all that you gain by becoming a man who honors God even when nobody is watching!

2. Think about our wives and the commitment we made when we stood before God and made vows of love and faithfulness to them. Betraying my wife for another woman, whether actual or virtual, is a thought that sickens me. Not in the sense that I'm above it or so holy that I could never do something like that, but in the sense that she would be utterly devastated and heartbroken. She loves me so much and trusts me so explicitly that to betray her in such a way would be an act of unthinkable cruelty.

Over the years, I have had occasional dreams of having been unfaithful to my wife. In these dreams I am desperately wishing I could undo what I've done. I'm begging for forgiveness from Cheryl, who is perplexed, crushed, and in total unbelief and despair. I'm telling her it was all a mistake and I really love her. Just at the moment that I can no longer bear the agony of having let down God and Cheryl and myself, I wake up, sometimes in a cold sweat. It takes a few minutes to come to the realization that it's all been a bad dream, a nightmare! However, when I fully come to my senses I begin to thank God that it was only a dream and not a reality. A few times I've been so elated that I've rolled over to hug and squeeze my lovely sleeping wife, who of course has no idea about the ordeal I've just gone through.

I honestly believe the Lord has allowed these dreams to warn me of the devastating consequences that would follow my yielding to the flesh.

3. *Think about your children.* One of the main characteristics of sexual sin is that the person is rendered irrational by their passions and is therefore no longer thinking about the consequences of their actions. As Solomon said,

> By means of a harlot [prostitute] a man is reduced to a crust of bread…Whoever commits adultery with a woman lacks understanding; he who does so destroys his own soul…Immediately he went after her, as an ox goes to the slaughter, or as a fool to the correction of the stocks [shackles]…Her house is the way to hell, descending to the chambers of death (Proverbs 6:26,32; 7:22,27).

I look at my children and realize that with one act of self-indulgence I could destroy their lives and potentially destroy their faith. They believe in me. They trust me. To some extent, they believe in Jesus because I taught them to. The thought of stumbling them is too much for me to handle. The thought of undoing all we've taught and established in their lives over the years is a price that's higher than I would ever want to pay. My older son tells his congregation (he's a pastor) that I'm his hero, his mentor, and the one who's taught him much of what he knows about the Lord. Would I throw all of that away for a moment's pleasure? God forbid!

Then there is my younger son. I sit with him to give him counsel and advice on life. I encourage him to follow Christ. Could he really take me seriously if my commitment to Christ couldn't keep me faithful to his mother? My daughters are beautiful young women. Am I willing to risk the possibility of their thinking of me as a pervert and a hypocrite? How could they ever hope to have a blessed marriage and a healthy relationship with their spouse if they, because of my sin and lust, cannot trust their own spouse to be faithful? No, these consequences are greater than I could bear. The price of sin is too high.

Before you begin to move in the direction of fulfilling the lust of your flesh, take a minute to think about the lives you will devastate and the God you will disgrace. Take an hour and review the life of David, who for a moment's pleasure with Bathsheba, another man's wife, reaped a lifetime of misery and strife. Eliminate sexual sin!

What Women Let Go Of

In 1996, Brian and I and our four children moved to England to serve the Lord at a newly formed church: Calvary Chapel Westminster, London. This move required quite a bit of liquidating. Our garage was brimming with items amassed over 13 years of living in the same community. There were limits on what we could take with us. Also, many of the household items we valued in America simply wouldn't work in England. We had to eliminate lamps, vacuums, electrical appliances, and anything else that would encumber us.

I'll never forget the garage sale I had with the kids. I stood and stared at many of our belongings spread out on the front lawn. Even at rock-bottom prices, the small vases and figurines I had treasured and kept for years couldn't even fetch a dime. Finally, I started giving those items away with each purchase. To my amazement, the patrons would return them, even removing them from their loaded bags with a sorry shake of the head. Our many accumulated items, big and small, had to be eliminated whether there was money to be gained or not. Our new life could not include everything we had accumulated over the years.

In like manner, in order to be able to enjoy a new life in Christ and the abundant and transformed marriage God intends you to have, there are behaviors, thoughts, and misconceptions that must be eliminated. The issues women have to release to God's care may be different than those our husbands must relinquish, but the struggles and the rewards can be very similar.

Eliminate Comparisons

Upon learning that a woman I was talking to was near my age, I began to study her face. The thought in my mind was, *Is that how many lines I have too?* I had immediately jumped to a comparison. I had to catch myself and simply say, *Stop it!*

Comparisons are false measurements. God calls us to measure our worth only by His absolute standard.

In the vaults of the International Bureau of Weights and Measures in Sevres, France, were formerly kept all the international prototypes—the true measures—of weight and height. Although most have been replaced by definitions based on physical constants, you will still find the original, prototype kilogram there. Whether defined by physical constant or an actual object, these are the ultimate standards. It is necessary to have them, or else weights and measures will begin to lose their precise values and accuracy—especially if they are compared only to other weights and measures, which could be false.

God is our true measure of all that is good and right and holy.

While preparing for a retreat, the event coordinators and I put my enthusiastic friend Dee in charge of cutting lengths of ribbon. As she got to talking with another helper, she began to measure each ribbon by the one previously cut rather than by the template piece. The 6-inch ribbon increased with each cut until the final ones measured over 12 inches! That's exactly what happens when we begin to compare our marriages or lives to those of others—we lose sight of exactly what we are aiming for! And that's God's best for you and me personally.

When you begin to compare your experience to that of others, you lose appreciation for what God has given you. It is easy to leap into discontent, frustration, and resentment. Have you ever stopped investing in what you have because you were wasting time and energy pining over your friend or neighbor's marriage? Have you ever tried to force your family into a certain mold because you were focusing on a worldly measure rather than on God's standard?

Praising God for Your Family's Foundation

In the time of Ezra the priest, the Jews who had returned from exile in Babylon set about to rebuild the temple to God. Much work was needed for this endeavor. The people labored removing rubble and clearing away a place to lay the foundation of the temple. After some time, it was laid. On the day of its dedication, some of the people cried while others shouted, and the outcome was confusion.

Those who cried did so because the new foundation looked so small compared to the first temple, built by King Solomon of Israel and destroyed by King Nebuchadnezzar of Babylon. Rather than rejoicing in the fact that God had allowed them to return to the land and once again have a place in their beloved Jerusalem, they chose to compare the foundation of this temple to the former grand temple of Solomon. Because of this spirit of comparison, those who had worked so hard were discouraged rather than celebratory. They were grumbling instead of singing praises.

When we compare our marriages to the relationships we get glimpses of at church, our community, or even on television, we become like those who cried at the foundation of the latter temple. We lament what we don't have, what we've lost, and what will never be. In the very midst of God working in our lives, we have the audacity to be unappreciative of what God is laying and building at that very moment.

I know how easy it is to slide into comparison mode and undermine my marriage. I recall one evening when I really turned from acknowledging God's work in our relationship and instead focused all my attention on the gap between Brian and me and a seemingly perfect couple. We were meeting this couple for dinner, but a heated altercation delayed my arrival. Brian and I had talked through our difficulty over the phone, so I showed up late and on my own. Upon being seated at the table, I sheepishly admitted, "I'm late because we were fighting—but you know what that's like."

The woman shook her head and gave me a blank stare.

I turned my gaze to the man. "You fight with your wife sometimes, don't you?" That same blank look crossed the husband's face. That is, until he turned to face his wife. He stared endearingly at her and said to me, "We never fight. Never."

I made eye contact with Brian, hoping to gain some support, but he just smiled. "Well," I confessed, "Brian and I do fight sometimes."

The couple looked sympathetically at my husband and just shook their heads sadly. For the rest of the meal and on the way home I felt low, worthless, and humiliated. Later that evening, still obsessed with the topic, I said to Brian, "I don't want to fight with you ever again. That couple doesn't fight."

Somewhat flippantly Brian replied, "Who cares? We fight and that's okay."

Out of a sense of exhaustion and defeat, I argued with him. I gave him as many reasons as I could as to why I was not going to engage in fighting or arguing ever again. Of course, I was doing precisely what I said I didn't want to do!

Brian calmly replied that the nature of our marriage included an occasional disagreement, and he rather enjoyed those times when his inclination to debate met with my passionate opinions. It was the way God created us. He told me he felt that God used our disagreements to sharpen and shape both of us.

It was then that I realized how destructive I was when I let myself compare our marriage to anything other than God's work and foundation in our marriage. This union I hold dear is of precious value to Him and to us. It was time for me to stop complaining, comparing, and grumbling and to use my days to celebrate *my* marriage and sing praises to God for the foundation He is forming daily.

A WORD TO THE WOMEN:

Eliminate Unreal Expectations

C Earlier in this chapter, Brian talked to the men about eliminating fantasy. Well, the same issue is a concern for women, but I like to call it "eliminating unreal expectations." Believe me, it is very much the same battle. We just bring our own past, hopes, and misconceptions to the scenario.

Every woman begins her marriage with certain expectations for her husband. We expect them to be interested and involved in every aspect of our lives. We expect them to know exactly what we want for our birthday—without being told. We expect them to listen intently to every word that falls from our lips and ask all the right questions so they can intimately know our hearts. We expect them to write love songs and poems in our absence to tell how desperately they missed us. Well, I hate to be the one to break it to you, but most men aren't geared that way!

Where do we get these notions? We get them from fictional heroes born of another woman's imagination. We get these ideals from songs that are written to attract women and get them to pay money to listen to them so the writer and singer are enriched financially. We get these ideas from movies where the men are always well-dressed, clean (even when they are perspiring), and without exception, dashing.

The truth is, men don't always smell so good, look so good, or act so good. And if they are dashing, it is usually out the door on their way to work, a baseball game, or the garage to putter around. But if we are honest, we expect men to have the qualities we ourselves fall short on. Which of us is perfect? A mind reader? An immortal beauty?

We need to accept our men the way God made them. You can still pray for your husband's growth. And you can rejoice when he is transformed according to God's purpose over the years.

But you also need to love and encourage him right where he is, how he is, and as who he is today.

Live in the Real World—And Love It

In order to eliminate unreal expectations it is necessary to eliminate the sources that feed us the lies about what life, love, and marriage are all about. This might include some movies, romance novels, celebrity or gossip websites, and anything else that makes you think that your husband should be other than he is. I must add that if these sources are presenting false expectations and definitions of love, they are hurting you individually as well. Those unreal standards or false versions of the "good life" will make you feel incompetent and shortchanged. They lead away from the abundance of what comes to you from God's truths.

I hate to admit this, but I used to be addicted to soap operas. (Don't tell my mother!) It was for a short period but long enough for some negative effects to infiltrate my behavior. During this time of indulging in these daytime dramas, I became hypercritical of Brian. Everything he did was upsetting to me. In the meantime, my mind was filled with the romantic but unreal images of afternoon television. One day it dawned on me that I was not thinking about what was true, noble, or pure—the standard given in the Word in Philippians 4:8-9. Rather, my imagination was filled with false images, and those images were stealing the joy of real things away from me.

I decided to do an experiment to see if the soap operas were causing my restless heart. I stopped watching the shows for a whole week. Sure enough, I found myself entering and thinking about real life around me. I stopped criticizing Brian and started enjoying him. I also realized all that I had to be grateful for in my version of life, because I became refocused on God's promises unfolding in my marriage and my family. I could see the truth without the mental and spiritual clutter of a pretend version of happiness. At that point, I gave up the soaps for good!

Know Your Husband, Love Your Husband

My friends often comment on how wonderful it is that Brian buys me just what I want for Christmas or my birthday. Amazing, isn't it? Well, I've got a secret. I tell him exactly what I want! I leave notes everywhere beginning weeks before my birthday. I reserve what I want at a certain store, and then he can go get it with ease and with confidence. I also tell the kids to remind Dad what it is that I want. Sometimes, I just take Brian right up to the item and say, "This is what I want."

Men can't read our minds when it comes to presents or our presence of mind! They need us to clarify what we are feeling or wanting. Hinting around that we need a hug doesn't work. Although we believe we are clearly indicating what we need, we are likely sending mixed signals. If we want a hug or sign of affection, but also want them to realize this all on their own in order to prove that they love us, we tend to distance ourselves and send unwelcoming signals. And the longer a husband goes without intuiting exactly what we are longing for, the angrier we become. The colder we become. The more our signals say "Stay away!"

Men tend to focus on one thing at a time. This means they can miss something obvious right in front of them. This seems utterly outrageous and odd to wives because we maneuver through a daily maze of thoughts and focuses in our multitasking minds. But over and over we witness this big difference between husbands and wives in action. If you send your husband to the refrigerator to get the butter, he might very possibly return to the table to report that you are all out. So you walk to the refrigerator, open the door, and reach for one of the *six cubes* of butter stacked on the right-hand shelf.

After we had lived 18 months in the same house in England, my daughter asked Brian to check to see if her jeans were dry. He walked up to the washing machine, opened the door, and declared, "I don't know what she's talking about. There aren't any jeans in there." I then walked past him to the dryer and pulled out the missing pair of jeans. Can you relate?

God made us differently so that between us both, as we are united, there could be a fullness of thought.

Women are intuitive, intimate, and interested. We add these virtues to our men. We are often their link to insight, intimacy, and interest in the world around them or the vital aspects of home life and faith life. We see what they miss. We bring them close. We ask the right questions and find out the missing information. And if we can see our important role as a wonderful part of our marriage's health and stability, we can embrace our value as godly women and wives.

What Do You Need to Eliminate?

If you're close to "normal," there are likely other addictions, thoughts, or misconceptions you need to eliminate from your heart, mind, and lifestyle if you are going to have a blessed marriage. Hebrews 12:1 speaks about laying "aside every weight, and the sin which so easily ensnares us" so we can run the race set before us with endurance.

We cannot specifically name the weights or sins that might be impeding the progress of your marriage, but it is very likely the Holy Spirit is bringing to your mind right now the very things that need to be eliminated. It might be a friend who is always criticizing your husband, it might be your own tendency to complain, it might be a place you frequent that brings temptation into your heart. Just as your marriage is totally unique, so are the things you need to eliminate. Don't compare. Don't ask yourself or God why you have to give those things up while others are allowed to hold on a bit longer. Simply, for the sake of a blessed marriage, lay them down.

Paul the apostle writes in Romans 13:14, "Put on the Lord Jesus Christ, and make no provision for the flesh, to fulfill its lusts." When we write about eliminating unhealthy influences from your marriage and lives, we are saying exactly what Paul said: Don't leave room to return to the things you are eliminating. Don't hide them for a time, don't pack them away, don't simply cease from practicing those things—eliminate them!

Pray and ask God to work with you to restore your understanding of His measure, His standards, and His priorities for your relationship as husband and wife. May your marriage become blessed and fulfilling, and may it be wholly placed on the foundation God is forming for your life together.

KNOWING IS GROWING

1. We covered a lot of territory in this chapter! Go back through the sections and mark areas that you want to discuss with your spouse or pray about specifically for your life.

2. What childish things do you each still hold on to? Think about this, and honor each other by listening as you each share what it is you are carrying with you from the past. This isn't a time to present your spouse with a list of his or her issues. This is a time for self-awareness and God-awareness. Focus on what areas you need to work on.

3. Discuss with each other how you viewed sex as you were growing up. Did you see sex as a trivial thing or an evil of the flesh? Or did you have an understanding of the beauty of this intimacy that God created for the pleasure and connection of husbands and wives? Reclaim the truth of God's gift of sexual intimacy. Let this truth help you commit to eliminating the fantasies, porn, faulty definitions, and all other deceptions that are barriers to a fulfilling, healthy sex life with one another.

4. What expectations or self-deceptions do you each need to let go of? If you don't want to express these aloud, spend time pondering this question, praying separately, and then praying for one another to have strength to embrace the goodness and potential of *real* life.

5. Discuss what you want to eliminate from your home that causes either of you or your children to stumble in your pursuit of faith, purity, and purpose. Simple changes can create a better environment. For example, place the family computer in an open area so nobody is tempted to pull up private, sexual material or communicate with anyone they aren't supposed to. (This will be a good move if you have kids! They are tempted more and more by website offerings.)

GROWING-TOGETHER GRACE

God, reveal to us all we cling to that is of no use to Your purpose and will. Give us strength to resist temptation and the heart to embrace Your promises and vision for a whole and loving marriage. Build in us the conviction we need to persevere in hard times, to compare ourselves and our marriage only *to Your measure, and to praise You for all You are doing in and through our union. Bless our marriage so that it might be a righteous and pleasing offering to You.*

Essential
THREE:

Esteem

Let marriage be held in honor (esteemed worthy,
precious, of great price, and especially dear).

Hebrew 13:4 amp

Esteem

The value of marriage in our culture has fallen on hard times. People used to hold it in high esteem. It was revered as sacred. But over time, an attitude of "Why bother?" or "What's the point?" has settled into our minds and hearts.

We used to hear people speak of their husband or wife, but today we hear co-workers, neighbors, and some friends speak of their "partner": a person they live with as though he or she is a spouse, but without the commitment or reverence of a marriage.

Many view marriage as nothing more than a social construct based on an outdated and obsolete value system, and they believe it should be replaced by something more relevant to today's tolerant and multicultural values. Same-sex marriage has now been declared a constitutional right by many lawmakers in the United States, and similar ideas are prevalent in Europe, Canada, Australia, New Zealand, and South Africa. Even some Latin American countries have embraced the idea.

Are these new perspectives right? Is there any reason to maintain the traditionally esteemed view of marriage? Is marriage just a human construct that we are free to adjust or dismiss as we see fit?

God has answers for us, and His Word and His wisdom show us how to respect and esteem marriage as He intended…and also *our* marriage as He intended.

How Does God Feel About Marriage?

B According to the Bible, marriage originated with God and must be understood in light of what He has to say on the subject. In the book of Genesis (the book of beginnings) we read,

> The LORD God said, "It is not good that man should be alone; I will make him a helper comparable to him"…And the LORD God caused a deep sleep to fall on Adam, and he slept; and He took one of his ribs, and closed up the flesh in its place. Then the rib which the LORD God had taken from the man He made into a woman, and He brought her to the man…Therefore a man shall leave his father and mother and be joined to his wife, and they shall become one flesh (Genesis 2:18,21-22,24).

God is the author of the marriage relationship and the One who presided over the first wedding ceremony. Jesus, when He condemned adultery and divorce, repeatedly taught that God is the author of marriage and also the One who set the bounds of marriage.

As God's creation, marriage is not to be tampered with by man. It is not to be replaced with something more culturally relevant, or redefined to suit the fancy of a sexually liberated society. Rather, it is to be held in the highest esteem and entered into with the deepest commitment. This is exactly what we are told in the New Testament: "Let marriage be held in honor (esteemed worthy, precious, of great price, and especially dear)" (Hebrews 13:4 AMP).

What the world thinks of marriage should be irrelevant to those of us who are followers of Jesus Christ. How others disrespect God's definition of and delight in marriage should break our hearts, but it should not change our hearts toward this perspective. We need to keep our focus on what God wants us to do in relation to the institution He established for our benefit and blessing.

A WORD TO THE MEN:

Straight Talk

B Men, what do you think of your marriage? Do you see it as a gift from God? What do you think of your wife? Do you see her as God's gift to you? Do you treat your relationship with your wife as a treasure to value and preserve?

I remember in the early years of married life getting together with guy friends and engaging in a little lighthearted wife-bashing and lamenting the "hardship" of keeping the marriage a happy one. We would jokingly tell stories of some of the strange things our wives would do. And, of course, we would talk about some of the unreasonable things they wanted us to do. Like go shopping with them at the mall all day; spend our day off doing chores around the house; take care of the kids so they could have an evening out with their friends; require us to shave, shower, and brush our teeth before we get in bed; and other irrational and outlandish things.

Although we considered it lighthearted, the wives didn't. I knew it was all done in fun, but I found that it really hurt Cheryl's feelings and caused her to question my love for her. I realized that by engaging in that kind of adolescent banter, I was failing to cherish the woman God had given me. I had to repent.

Marriage Is a Stewardship

Again, do you see your wife as someone God has entrusted to your care? Proverbs 18:22 declares, "He who finds a wife finds a good thing, and obtains favor from the LORD." Do you realize you've been given a stewardship in your marriage that you'll one day be called to give an account for? (If you're not familiar with the idea of stewardship, wait for just a moment.)

Frankly, I don't think most men see marriage the way God sees it, and this lack of understanding causes many problems in many marriages. Is yours one of those marriages that is suffering from a lack of esteem? Does it shock you or overwhelm you with guilt to know that marriage is a stewardship that God has entrusted to you?

I think that even the concept of stewardship is very remote. We've lost the language of sanctity and responsibility to one another in our very me-focused culture. It'd be nice to say that this has happened only in the secular realm, but it just isn't so. I don't know anyone who hasn't at one point or another struggled with overfeeding their ego, insisting on their own way, or looking out for their gain rather than God's.

In Roman times, when the Bible was written, a steward was the general manager over all of his master's affairs and possessions. In writing to the Corinthians, Paul referred to himself as a steward of the mysteries of God, and then said, "It is required in stewards that one be found faithful" (1 Corinthians 4:1-2). In general, stewards highly esteemed their masters and would fulfill their duties with the utmost diligence and care.

If you and I began to adopt the view that we are stewards of our marriages, how would this change our behaviors, focus, and priorities? Dramatically! Let's look at what the steward's perspective is.

1. God is my master; I am His servant. When you place God as your one and only master, you eliminate the self-permission to serve yourself first. Your marriage is about a lot more than your joy and contentment! That would shock a lot of guys. Many leave their family home and move on to marriage with the hope they'll be taken care of, served, and adored as head of the household. They have forgotten who the true head of the household is—God almighty.

2. My wife, my marriage, my family, and whatever else I have, belong to God. Since all I am and have really is the Lord's possession, I must manage His things with absolute diligence and faithfulness.

It's easy at times to take our wives for granted. That's why Paul, by the Spirit, said, "Husbands ought to love their own wives as their own bodies…For no one ever hated his own flesh, but nourishes and cherishes it" (Ephesians 5:28-29). We are to see our wives as a true extension of ourselves and care for them as we care for our own well-being.

Every day I make sure I'm well-fed, well-clothed, well-groomed, well-treated, and so on…but do I do that for my wife? I make sure that my interests are given the full attention that's needed, and if anyone dares to interfere, I'm really good at blocking that interference! What about my commitment to anything that serves the interests of my wife or the things that promote the well-being of my marriage? Men, unless we commit to God's perspective and priority on marriage we'll never attain the blessing He intends in this relationship. Let marriage be held in honor—esteemed worthy, of great value.

Undivided Esteem

When I talk about esteeming your marriage, I'm really guiding you to esteem your wife. You can't, with any integrity, say that you greatly value your marriage and simultaneously disrespect or mistreat your wife. And to just say, "I esteem my wife" is not good enough—you need to show it.

Let me give a few examples of things we should never do if we are to put our actions behind our words.

1. We should never, under any circumstances, be physically abusive to our wives. No sane man intentionally abuses his own body. Therefore, we should never abuse our wives. This should go without saying, but sadly, it needs to be reinforced. Over the years I have spoken to or been involved with counseling or helping Christian couples who were dealing with physical abuse. Men, this is absolutely unacceptable. Remember that your wife is not your property; she belongs to God and is yours to care for and nurture and protect. If you are the one she is needing protection from, then you must seek help immediately.

2. We should never emotionally abuse our wives. There is such a thing as emotional abuse. Maybe you've never lifted your hand to harm your wife but you abuse her with your behavior, attitudes, and words. Do you play mind games with her? Are you passive-aggressive? You are demonstrating this if you act nonchalant about a situation or a decision and then make your wife pay for it by sulking, becoming angry about other things, or making degrading remarks about her or her role in the situation.

Did you know that by checking out or flirting with other women, you are causing your wife emotional harm? Some men engage in this behavior because they want their wife to know that there are plenty of other options if she doesn't toe the line or treat him right. Whether this is your intention or not, you are presenting a threat to your wife and to your union when you do this. There isn't anything fun about that.

Comments about another woman or sideways glances at a passing woman play on a wife's insecurities and fears. Fears of not being good enough, fears of not being truly loved, fears of being set aside for someone prettier, younger, thinner, smarter. This kind of abuse is pure wickedness born out of a sick male ego, and it has no place in marriage. This is not only childish, it is downright sinful and absolutely wrong—and God who searches the heart knows what we are doing and will hold us accountable.

3. Never verbally abuse your wife. There's no place in a Christian marriage for screaming at the top of our lungs, name-calling, or using vulgar or obscene language when speaking to our wives or to anyone. Do you flip a switch and turn on the anger when something doesn't go your way? Or do you hold on to complaints and problems and let them fester until you explode? I'd say that many of us fall into one of those camps unless we get our emotions in check and our hearts in line with God's peace.

We will have disagreements in marriage. But we don't have to raise our voices or cross the line of decency by using destructive speech. God warns us against such language in His Word: "Let no corrupt word proceed out of your mouth, but what is good for necessary edification, that it may impart grace to the hearers" (Ephesians 4:29).

In all the arguments and shouting matches Cheryl and I have had over the years, I've never sworn at her or called her a vulgar or obscene name. That is a line you simply never cross as a Christian husband. I'm not saying that to sound "holier than thou" or to condemn someone who has done that. I'm saying it so you'll know that God is able to give sufficient grace and power to overcome those kinds of things.

Before I was a Christian, my speech was belligerent, profane, and obscene most of the time. God took that kind of language away from me upon my conversion, and I believe He'll do the same for anyone who desires Him to. I must admit I've been shocked at times to hear about some of the things guys have said to their wives. I have said to men I've counseled, "Don't you realize that God is watching how you treat your wife? That God is listening to the way you're talking to her? That God hears the things you're saying?"

Men, this is where we need to remember the warning of Jesus that for every idle word men speak they will give an account of it in the Day of Judgment (Matthew 12:36). That is not just a threat—it's an absolute promise. Verbal abuse can be just as destructive to a person's soul and spirit as physical abuse can be to the body because, as Proverbs 18:21 says, "Death and life are in the power of the tongue." I've sat in counseling sessions and listened to heart-wrenching stories from women about the abusive things their husbands have said to them. This should never be the case with Christian men. The man who truly esteems his marriage and cherishes his wife will never be verbally abusive.

A WORD TO THE WOMEN:

Embracing an Eternal View of Marriage

C I get so mad at the idea of buying an extended warranty on every appliance. It seems nothing is built to last anymore. Instead of guaranteeing the product, the seller is basically guaranteeing that your appliance *will* break down. Then what will you do without that special extra plan that costs almost as much as the washer you just bought?

In the same manner, many soon-to-be-marrieds now insist on prenuptial agreements. What's that, if not insurance for when the whole thing breaks down?

We live in a disposable generation. Everything is for temporary use, and after it has served its purpose, it can simply be discarded. Not so with marriage. God built marriages to last a lifetime. We are to esteem our marriage by placing it on a higher plane than any other institution.

During a women's retreat I attended as a speaker, a woman from the audience rose to her feet to address the audience during a time of sharing. With tears in her eyes and a strained voice, she warned the other women. She talked about the time when she had had a beautiful house, a loving husband, and four children underfoot. During that time, a dashing man entered her life. She struck up a friendship with this man and would often complain to him when she felt unappreciated at home. He sympathized with her and told her of his own unhappiness. Soon an intimate relationship developed between them. This man convinced her to leave her husband and family and run away with him. She did.

It was the greatest regret of her life. It was only after her seductor had left her for another woman that she fully recognized her folly. She was estranged from all four of her children. It seemed they still couldn't forgive her for abandoning them and hurting their father. Her first husband still harbored anger at her for what she had done to her family emotionally.

As this broken woman stood before the assembly, she began to shake. She confessed her own bitterness at the circumstances of her life. She was angry at her decisions and stupidity. She missed her children. She herself was now abandoned, alone, and working hard to simply survive.

She sat down after her confession but raised her hand a few minutes later. I called on her again, "Could someone please help me?" she said in a strained voice. "I think I'm having a heart attack!" Quickly we called the nurses in the audience to her side. The rest of the assembly exited the building while the paramedics were summoned. The woman was taken to the hospital, where it was confirmed that she had suffered a heart attack.

One of my friends waited for her in the hospital. The woman felt even more obligated to pour out her heart after her ordeal. She spoke endlessly about her estranged children and the wonderful marriage and life she had destroyed. She lamented how she wished she had realized then what it meant to hold her marriage as sacred.

I believe she taught the greatest lesson of all to us that weekend. Every one of us went home with renewed thanksgiving for our marriages, our children, and our homes. And I believe that many women went home with a conviction of the heart. How easy it is to complain about your life or fall into a rut in your marriage and then look for a way out! When we start looking elsewhere, or place our faith and worth elsewhere, then we stop investing in our home life. A marriage will not grow and mature in good ways if love, attention, and commitment are withheld.

Honor Your Marriage

Many women ask me, "How do you honor your marriage in practical ways?"

Well, first I revere it. I don't demean it. When I was a young pastor's wife (now I am a middle-aged one…sort of), I would sometimes criticize my marriage as a way to connect with or somehow encourage women I was counseling.

For instance, when counseling a single woman, I would tell her all the hard places in marriage, including my own struggles. I often exaggerated them to make her feel better about her singleness.

I was afraid that in displaying the happiness of my marriage, I might make someone feel bad about her own marriage. So to the unhappily married woman I often overplayed my own issues or lumped poor Brian in with the hapless man she was married to. One day the Lord caught me in the act. I felt the Holy Spirit nudging me: *What are you doing?* I answered in part that I was trying to make the person I was addressing feel better about everything.

The Lord spoke to me right then and there about esteeming my marriage. Rather than encouraging the suffering women I spoke to, I was discouraging them. I was not giving them an example to follow or a godly standard of what marriage was supposed to be. Instead I was telling them there was *no* marriage that was worthwhile. Oops!

I prayed about the approach I had been taking. I asked the Lord for His forgiveness. My counseling times changed drastically. I began to share about the beauty of my own marriage, and found I became rather inspirational. What do you know?

In our women's Bible study, one of the exercises we were asked to do during the week was to write down ten things we were thankful for in our marriage. Though I found that question delightful, I had a dear friend who was struggling to complete that assignment when she got home. Each reason for thanksgiving required much thought and concentration to dredge up. Her marriage was in a bad state. After struggling to write nine answers, she was so frustrated that she left her notebook on the dining-room table and headed out. She didn't return home until much later, and the scene she encountered shocked her.

Walking in, she found her husband at the table. He was holding her answers in his hand. Tears were brimming in his eyes. "Do you mean what you wrote? Are you really thankful for me?" She answered honestly that she had meant every word she wrote. Her list so moved him that he apologized for not being a better husband to her. He vowed to change and to do better. She returned to the study with a full heart and a completed list. It seemed her esteem of her marriage had moved her husband's heart.

Though esteeming your marriage won't always bring such speedy results, it is nevertheless worth the effort and thought. Even if you get frustrated. Even if you have to dig deep in the beginning, a list like this could really change your heart. And who knows, maybe it will change the heart of your spouse as well.

Another woman I know was married to a man who was grumpy for 50 years of their marriage. And then he had an amazing encounter with God. His whole demeanor radically changed. He became one of the most jovial and kind men ever. After 10 years of joy he died.

The wife confided to me that the final years of their marriage had been well worth the 50 she had struggled through. Not only that, but her children were given a wonderful example of grace by their loving mother and saw God answer her prayers in a wonderful way.

Protect Your Marriage

Protecting my marriage is part of esteeming it. I guard it by avoiding social interaction with other men when my husband is not around. I might have an occasional conversation, but it stops there. I don't want to ever open any doors to inappropriate emotions or a relationship that could potentially bring harm. My friendships with men are through the auspices of my husband. Even if I have a male friend through work or through my family relationships, I consider that person "our" friend rather than my friend.

I also watch out for other women. Myself, I think my husband looks a lot like Cary Grant. Unfortunately, so do other women. I can tell when one of them approaches him with that look that says, *I'd like you to be more than my pastor.*

A woman once had the audacity to come up to me and tell me she was dreaming about my husband! I recall telling her that the devil was trying to adulterate the love of Jesus she had for her pastor. She didn't buy it. I felt sorry for her, but I sure wasn't going to turn her over to Brian!

I warn Brian about situations like that one, but I don't blame him for being cute. That's just the way God made him. However, I do remind him how much I love him and how he is God's special gift to me. I also pray for him to be strong in the Lord and the power of His might.

It is not wrong—rather, it's very wise—to be protective of the marriage God has given you. Remind your husband how much you have together, and how much you love him. My mom used to say, "A man wants to be where he is most admired and wanted." I try to make that place our home.

Setting Up Boundaries

C Brian and I have placed certain safeguards around our marriage. We call these borders. Whereas we used to have people over and in our house all the time, we now tend to be very selective and seldom in our invitations. We have found that we need to guard our time together.

When Brian is home, I keep my phone conversations short and to a minimum. My friends now start the conversation with "Is Brian with you?" They know if I am with him, I don't have the time to talk. He needs my attention.

I was talking to a friend in her kitchen, when her husband came in the door. "Cheryl," he announced, "I need some time alone with my wife." She smiled at me sheepishly. I returned a wide grin and told them both that I totally understood.

I went into another room where I could hear the husband pouring out his hard day to his wife. I could also hear her understanding responses.

By the time we were all seated at the dinner table, the husband was composed and comforted. He was again restored to the headship of his family and assured of his wife's undiminished support and love. I was impressed.

Respect Your Spouse

In 1967, Aretha Franklin recorded the song "R-E-S-P-E-C-T," and it was an instant hit! But the original version was written and recorded in 1965 by Otis Redding. This song that struck a chord in thousands of listeners was born of a man's desire for a little respect from his loved one. Men want to be respected. And so do we!

Like all kids, I learned the playground adage, "Sticks and stones may break my bones, but words will never hurt me." But it didn't take me long to realize that it simply wasn't true. Mean names and accusations *do* hurt my feelings. Sometimes wounded feelings hurt worse than broken bones!

There are few people who can ignore a mean comment. It seems that mean words stay with us longer and more strongly than kind ones. Women are weak in arguments. We are not as strong as men. They seem so determined to do what we have asked them not to do. But we are great at saying mean things. When we feel like we are losing, we go to our last arsenal, the arsenal of mean words. We throw every bomb we find in the ammunition chest without reading the label or thinking about the damage that will follow. We do, however, think about the initial jolt that names like "jerk" and "idiot" have. In the heat of the moment, they are heart-stopping insults. In the long term, they are demeaning.

Jesus said in Matthew 7:12, "Whatever you want men to do to you, do also to them, for this is the Law and the Prophets." In other words, treat others as you want to be treated. As women, we want to be treated with respect…but are we treating our spouse with respect?

One day after praying for a little more respect, God allowed me to hear my own tone of voice when I addressed Brian. I was horrified. Clearly I hadn't taken time to listen to myself or I would have detected this awful tone much earlier. And if I wasn't listening to me, why should my husband? I understood why I wasn't receiving respect: In order to get respect, you must give respect.

Infusing our speech and attitude with respect when we address our spouse will honor them and our marriage. When we esteem our marriage we see it as God sees it—worthy of all our respect.

Reasons to Esteem Your Marriage

God desires that we esteem our marriage because He is the author of the marriage relationship, but what did He have in mind when he invented it? Does the Bible give an answer to that question? Yes, it does. It seems clear that there are at least three reasons why God created marriage.

One of those reasons is procreation. God said to Adam and Eve, "Be fruitful and multiply." However, men and women are not animals, preprogrammed to mate merely for the purpose of producing more off-spring. Men and women are creatures made in God's image, who are to reproduce within a loving, committed relationship to one another. In this way they bring their offspring into an environment of love, respect, and security. Marriage produces the ideal environment for the reproduction and nurturing of human life.

Another reason God invented marriage is so that through the marriage relationship, men and women could experience in some sense the love God has for His people. That is what Paul meant when he said, "'A man shall leave his father and mother and be joined to his wife, and the two shall become one flesh.' This is a great mystery, but I speak concerning Christ and the church" (Ephesians 5:31-32).

But there's one more reason God invented marriage—and this, we believe, is the primary reason. Marriage was to provide man with *companionship*. When God surveyed His creation He saw one area where things were still incomplete. "And the LORD God said, 'It is not good that man should be alone; I will make him a helper comparable to him'" (Genesis 2:18).

Companionship is what God had in mind when He invented marriage. Sometimes as Christians we can spiritualize things to the point that we forget that God intends to bless us on the natural level as well as the spiritual level. Some people think that to say He created marriage for companionship is downright "worldly." Somehow they've lost sight of the fact that He created men and women with emotions and feelings, and with the capacity to laugh and have fun and actually enjoy the good things in life. There are those who say that a husband and wife should not have sex simply for the pleasure of it, without the intent of producing a child. They believe that to do so is downright sinful! But this thinking contradicts what God tells us here in Genesis and is actually more Gnostic than Christian.

The Gnostics, who derived many of their views from the Greek philosophers, believed that whatever of the material world was essentially evil and only that which was spirit was pure. These ideas made their way into the church not long after the apostolic period and have even found their way down to us today. We've seen this thinking process appear subtly in many places in the church, but the one place in particular is in premarital counseling sessions. The conversation goes something like this:

Counselor: So you want to get married?

Couple: Well, we think so. But we're not sure if it's God's will.

Counselor: Fair enough. You definitely want to be in God's will, so let's talk about that. Let me ask you a few questions. First, do you love each other?

Couple: We haven't talked much about that. We thought we should just pray instead.

Counselor: Um, okay. Are you attracted to each other?

Couple: Well, kind of, but we're concerned that we might be in the "flesh." And we know that God doesn't want us focusing on outward appearances but on the heart. So we just try not to think about those things.

Counselor: Hmm…okay. Do you two like each other? Are you friends?

Couple: What's that got to do with it? We worry that if we are physically attracted to one another, like to have fun together, and feel that we are in love, then it most likely would be the flesh driving us together. Those can't be of God, right?

Wrong! The Bible tells us that God has given us richly all things to enjoy. Over the years we've heard these kinds of things over and over again. What this tells us is that we who are church leaders, pastors, and teachers have failed to clearly communicate God's primary objective for marriage. Which, we remind you again, is companionship! Companionship! Companionship! Spiritual companionship. Mental companionship. Emotional companionship. Physical companionship.

We esteem God's purpose for marriage when we embrace the

wholeness and fullness of these four areas. We'll briefly look at each of these categories and describe how we embrace them personally.

Spiritual Companionship

It is very important to become an encourager of our spouse's faith. In our marriage, we have learned to pray together and share God's Word with each other so we are creating a strong spiritual foundation.

What do you have in common spiritually with your husband or wife? Do you strive to grow together, or are you only increasing your faith knowledge separately? Small Bible-study or discussion groups that are geared to just men or just women are very healthy. But don't forget to grow as a couple. Prayer, reading Scripture, praying for one another, and incorporating God's love and purpose into your family conversations will strengthen this area of your companionship.

Brian: Cheryl is my partner in my calling and my greatest source of encouragement in the faith. When making major decisions I'm always anxious to get her perspective on things. When I'm considering different aspects of ministry or even when I'm meditating on a passage of Scripture, I love to sit down with her and get her insight. I know she has a deep relationship with the Lord and I depend on her wisdom frequently.

Cheryl: We work and serve side by side and enjoy discussing and debating doctrine and theology. We love missions and missionary stories. We pass missionary biographies back and forth between us. We hold strong convictions about ministry and long to see God work powerfully in our generation. We are each other's spiritual confidant.

Mental Companionship

Finding common ground and common interests will help any marriage become more stable and more enjoyable. When you can respect each other's area of wisdom or expertise or even intuition, then you reach a deeper level of mental companionship. We know that many couples struggle because they have become too independent in their lives. They aren't sharing and listening to one another with generous attention and care. You don't have to both love science. But if one of you can't wait to share about an article on a new discovery, the other should invest in their spouse's joy and share in the exchange of ideas. This takes some patience and deliberate effort. But the mental companionship, when nurtured, is one of the great keys to helping one another feel loved and esteemed.

Brian: Cheryl is brilliant. I love her mind. We talk together about history, politics, science, literature, entertainment, and a hundred other things. She is a voracious reader and has a retention level of probably 99 percent. She never ceases to amaze me with her knowledge of facts about food, nature, celebrities, words and their definitions, and so on. When I scratch my head and say, "How *does* she know all that?" it is out of pure admiration and respect!

Cheryl: We love Europe and especially England, so we love to watch British films, documentaries, and mysteries. It's such a treat to cozy up with Brian and watch a movie that sparks conversation about our enthusiasm over England. It's such a simple thing, but it draws us closer because we appreciate this area of sharing.

Emotional Companionship

When we talk about emotional companionship, we are referring to the relational aspect of marriage. Some have described it in terms of having a soul mate, someone you connect with on that deep emotional level. Apart from that deep spiritual connection through our relationship with Christ, this is the area where we discover the joy of marriage day to day.

Brian: Not only is Cheryl brilliant mentally, she's stimulating emotionally. She is intense. She's a woman of deep conviction. She's energetic. She's caring and compassionate. Over the years I've battled with a physical ailment that has sent me into seasons of deep depression. During those times Cheryl has always been there to pray for me and to speak that word in season to my weary soul. She has been a wise counselor indeed.

She can also make me laugh like nobody else can. One of her funniest routines is to carry on a dialogue between the two of us with her doing both parts. She will often ask me a question that I either don't respond to, or respond to too quietly for her to hear me, and that will send her into one of these routines. The words she puts in my mouth are absolutely hilarious. Nowadays, I will intentionally ignore her when she asks me a question just for the sheer pleasure of hearing her go into the routine. She's amazingly spontaneous! I love it.

Cheryl: There is so much that Brian and I share together. No one gets as excited as we do over the accomplishments of our children and grandchildren. There are times we answer each other with a phrase one of our children used to employ. We know what we are saying and what it means. It is a secret, shared code between us, and we cherish it.

Brian is the one I bare my heart to with confidence. He listens to my tirades and complaints, and never judges me by the words I say in the heat of the trial. I love that!

Recently I was telling a friend about an incident involving one of our grandsons. When he was three he was intrigued with car key alarms. Finding what looked like a car key alarm in my nightstand he pushed the colorful buttons. The effect was wailing sirens throughout the house. We all jumped to attention. Brian was gone at the time and hadn't relayed the alarm code to me.

Suddenly, through a speaker located by the alarm panel on a downstairs wall, an authoritative voice demanded to know the alarm code or the police would be dispatched. I tried to explain to the voice that my grandson had inadvertently set off the alarm. The voice was not convinced. He demanded the secret word. I began to repeat every word I could imagine Brian using for an alarm code. Finally I said the right one. Satisfied, the voice congratulated me, and the alarms stopped blaring.

After the incident, I hid the alarm remote from my grandson. However, he wasn't the only one who couldn't find it. I forgot where I put it! My friend asked if Brian had been upset. Truth is, he showed me a ton of grace, and he does so regularly.

Brian's demonstration of complete grace is a model for me. I am not the perfect wife. I don't have the perfect body. I don't always display the perfect attitude, but my husband's grace is unconditional. He doesn't judge me by what I did yesterday. Every day is a fresh start. He provides me emotional support and freedom to be me.

Physical Companionship

If we esteem our marriages, if we see marriage not as a human construct, but as God's institution and gift to men and women to bless them, we will experience a greater intimacy in all areas of our relationships. Sharing physical intimacy with your helpmate, partner, and life love brings great pleasure and harmony to a marriage.

> Blessed is every one who fears the LORD, who walks in His ways…Your wife shall be like a fruitful vine in the very heart of your house, your children like olive plants all around your table. Behold, thus shall the man be blessed who fears the LORD (Psalm 128:1-4).

Brian: Cheryl is absolutely beautiful. She was beautiful the first time I saw her over 30 years ago and she's just as beautiful today. Sometimes I look at her and think, *I can't believe she's my wife!* She really loves that I tell her every day she's beautiful, but honestly, it's not difficult to do. I'm not making it up—she really is gorgeous!

Cheryl: Brian is my best friend, soul mate, and the love of my life. I don't think I realized how special he was when I first married him. Honestly, I was taken with his handsome face and kind demeanor. It's only as the years have progressed and we have persevered through a few storms that I have realized what a great prize God gave me.

The other day, Brian knew I had a tough meeting to attend. During the middle of it I received a text on my phone. I read, "I didn't get the chance this morning to tell you that I love you and that you look beautiful. I am praying for you. Love, Brian." It was just the word I needed at just the right time.

Brian listens, shows me grace, and makes me feel secure in his love. His generous words and actions have helped me grow and become a more gracious and godly woman.

I still thrill when he walks through the door every evening. I usually have a ton of things I have saved up during the day to tell him about. I also love to hear about his adventures during the day. This fellowship we share as best friends has created an intimate bond between us that I treasure and enjoy.

Take time to look at each area of your marriage to determine where it is healthy or unhealthy, godly or ungodly, nurtured or neglected. When you esteem your marriage, your focus will be on causing it to grow daily in the direction of God's will and way.

KNOWING IS GROWING

1. Discuss God's view of marriage. How do you and don't you give marriage the respect God intended?

2. Discuss how the world's declining esteem of marriage has affected your attitudes and behaviors. Think about practical ways you and your spouse can reclaim reverence and honor for and in your marriage?

3. How do you like to be shown respect? Discuss this with your spouse. You might have similar ways of "hearing" respect, or you might find that you need to receive it in very different ways. Have a conversation and discover how to R-E-S-P-E-C-T your loved one.

4. Separately, each of you write a list of ten things you are grateful for in relation to your marriage. Share these and talk about them.

5. Commit to nurturing the four areas of companionship. How have these areas been supported or neglected in your marriage? Diligently seek ways to grow together spiritually, mentally, emotionally, and physically. Put ideas into practice and bring balance to the four areas.

GROWING-TOGETHER GRACE

Lord, grant us Your heart for the holy union of marriage. Help us to esteem our relationship by honoring You and one another. Remind us of all we have to be grateful for. As we extend grace and love to each other, help us to show respect for our differences as well as our areas of common ground. Strengthen our resolve to avoid going through the motions as we listen to one another and say the words, "I love you" sincerely and frequently. Bless this marriage, Lord.

Essential
FOUR:

Encourage

Whatever you want men to do to you, do also to them.

MATTHEW 7:12

Encourage

Every couple wants to have a good marriage. But we mustn't forget that marriage in and of itself is neither good nor bad. As consumers, we like to think in terms of getting something and then assessing its value. We weigh whether it's a good or bad product or service. But we don't purchase a marriage off the shelf and then evaluate whether we got a good one or a lemon! Our marriages will be good or bad depending on *how* and *what* we invest in them.

If that feels like an overwhelming responsibility, keep in mind that it is indeed a responsibility, but when we turn to God's Word and leading, it will not be an overwhelming task but a joy. He knows what our marriages need in order to be good, joyful, and fruitful unions, and He's laid it out clearly in His Word. Yet we must actually heed His guidance.

Are you ready as a couple to follow God's leading? Are you ready to turn your marriage into a good and blessed union that serves God, your family, and others? It is possible. If you add to your union a bit of encouragement and a willingness to commit to a labor of love, you will experience all that God has purposed marriage to be.

Does Your Wife Know She Is Loved?
Does Your Husband Know He Is Loved?

 During lunch, my friend Carol seemed troubled. When we got in the car afterward, I asked her what was concerning her. She looked at me kindly and inquired, "Is everything all right between you and Brian?"

"Of course!" I responded rather offhandedly. I then went on to list a number of ways I was proving what a great wife I was to him. I was homeschooling his children. I was teaching Sunday school at his church. I was helping and serving the women in his congregation. I was living in England, half a world away from my parents, friends, and security. I was hosting his friends regularly at our house. I was doing his laundry. I was fixing his meals. I was entertaining his guests. Of course everything between Brian and me was great!

Carol is one of the godliest and most perceptive women I know. My rambling list of good credentials seemed to make her more uncomfortable. She looked me in the eye. "Does Brian *know* that you love him and you support him?"

I thought that was an odd question to ask. Hadn't she heard my great résumé? I replied that he *must* know I loved him because of all I was doing for him.

"Have you told him lately that you love him or that you support him?" She probed a bit deeper.

The honest answer was that I hadn't. I had just assumed that all my activity and effort on his behalf would show him I loved him.

Carol left me with a sweet encouragement to tell my husband I loved him that night.

Later in the evening, Brian and I were alone doing the dishes. "Brian," I ventured, "you know that I love you, right?"

He turned to me with sincerity in his eyes and responded, "Do you?"

"What do you mean by that!" I shot back. I launched into my handy enumeration of all the things I did for him, reinforcing the evidence of my love.

"I thought you were doing those for Jesus," he said.

Now I was feeling convicted. My harping on the duties of devotion felt like the sounding brass and clanging cymbals of 1 Corinthians 13. Worthless. All noise. It was not profiting me, and it clearly was not reflecting the love I thought it did to Brian. I told him about my conversation with Carol.

"She's right," he agreed. I was astounded. After years of marriage and four children, how could he doubt my love? Yet he did doubt, because in my busyness I had neglected to take time to say, "I love you. We're in this together."

After I apologized, Brian opened up his heart to me and we talked for a long time. I learned a valuable lesson that day. It was the lesson of encouraging my marriage.

A WORD TO THE WOMEN:

How to Encourage Your Marriage

C I have often heard women complain that their husbands aren't pulling their weight. They will ask me, "Isn't marriage supposed to be fifty-fifty?" The short answer is "no." Marriage is rarely fifty-fifty. Things in life just don't divide up that evenly.

Sometimes marriage is a ratio of ten to ninety. Other times it is more like twenty-five to seventy-five. Not always are the percentages on the man's side. There are times when I realize my husband is doing a lot more for the encouragement of our marriage than I am.

Brian likes to say that if the women concentrated on their part—"Wives, submit to your husbands as unto the Lord"— and the men on theirs—"Husbands, love your wives, just as Christ also loved the church and gave Himself for her"—most marital problems would disappear. The problem is, husbands and wives are overoccupied with the other's role.

Women approach me all the time with the complaint, "My husband isn't loving me as Christ loved the church." Of course, their husbands are usually complaining to Brian that their wives aren't submissive or respectful. What's the problem here? Everybody is concentrating on everybody else's role.

When I was in fourth grade I helped direct and starred in a school production called *Dorothy and the Wizard of Oz.* Our lion kept forgetting her lines. I was so focused on feeding her the lines she was to say that at one point I completely forgot my own!

I think that is often what happens in marriage. We are so focused on what our partner is supposed to be doing or saying or becoming that we forget what *we* are supposed to be doing.

Much of our role in encouraging our marriage is to simply do our part…and do it wholeheartedly.

Submission as God Intended

To a lot of women *submission* is an ugly word. It conjures up thoughts of male dominance, control, and even abuse. But all that isn't the "submission" the Bible teaches. Those warped versions come from people, not God. The biblical word means to "come under the authority of." It is about leadership rather than dominance. Submission is to give the role of leadership to the husband.

Years ago, Brian and I had an ongoing argument about my role of submission. He claimed I never had to face the issue of submitting because I always agreed with him. Therefore I was *cooperative* rather than submissive. I argued that my cooperation was a sign of my submission. (Of course I was right!) Alas, submission has nothing to do with being right or wrong. It doesn't mean that you always agree with your husband's decisions or that you cannot voice objections. It means that at the end of the day he makes the final decision. This role of submission makes the first essential of entrustment—praying for your husband—even more essential. He is going to need wisdom and divine guidance to safeguard you and the family's welfare.

It's not like I haven't struggled with the concept of submission. I have. During my wedding, my father, who presided over the ceremony, stressed the word *obey* in the vows I was told to repeat. I remember looking at him beseechingly as if to say, *Don't make me say that!* He looked at me sternly and repeated, "Obey." Dad knew that if my marriage to Brian was going to last, I was going to have to give him the place of leadership in the home.

About three years ago, it all came to a head. Brian and I were struggling with a pretty serious issue. We both had strong opinions on how to deal with the situation, and our opinions did not agree. I saw what my husband could not see. I sensed what he could not sense. Every time I tried to communicate what I feared, he accused me of being rash and judgmental. Every discussion turned into an argument. We were both very concerned and passionate about the issue.

In utter frustration, after yet another heated argument, I took off to the beach. I remember Brian asking me if I wanted him to accompany me. I told him that I was not safe for him to be around—and I meant it. I was really angry.

I parked down at the beach and donned my walking shoes. I walked an impassioned pace for over ten miles. I complained to God the entire time. I ranted and raged in my mind about the whole thing. I explained to God my frustration and what I saw and what Brian couldn't see.

The Lord indicated to me that I was to go home and yield the leadership in this situation to my husband. "But Lord, he's absolutely wrong," I countered.

Gently the Lord brought to mind the passage in Mark 3:24-25: "If a kingdom is divided against itself, that kingdom cannot stand. And if a house is divided against itself, that house cannot stand."

God was reminding me that if I did not give Brian the lead in this situation, our house was sure to fall. However, if I would be obedient to Him in submitting to Brian, He would intervene and work with my husband and in the situation. The real issue was not so much submitting to Brian, but submitting to God and in doing so giving the leadership to Brian.

I was so engrossed in my argument with God that I ended up miles away from my car. But after He spoke to me, I understood what I needed to do. As I made the long walk back, I asked Him for the strength and grace to submit to my husband in this situation.

When I got home, I told Brian about my talk with the Lord. I told him how I didn't agree with the way he was leading in the issue, but that I would submit. It was less than a week later that the whole truth of the situation was exposed. When Brian came to see the entire picture, he led us beautifully through some very troubled waters. I realized that my submission at that critical point had been part of what had brought the final breakthrough.

If you are having a battle of the wills or the sexes at home, and you just can't let go of the control because you are *sure* you are right, remember that the one you are neglecting to submit to is your God. (And you thought the argument over the messy garage, or the kids' education, or your vacation plans was all about you and your husband!)

Paul the apostle, when talking about submission, is quick to add "as unto the Lord." Why? Because submission is about doing marriage *God's* way. We give husbands the leadership in the home because God said to give them the leadership.

This does not mean that the wife cannot initiate prayer, do Bible studies, teach the kids, or offer suggestions or advice. It simply means that she allows the husband to drive the car in the marriage. She might tell him where to turn now and then, but he is driving. It works!

Investing in Your Marriage

C There are numerous ways to invest in and encourage your marriage. And many will feel more like second nature to you than submission initially does. For example, I think women are great at investing time and energy. We seem to naturally assume the responsibilities of transforming the house into a home, doing the laundry, and cleaning the house and keeping order. Unfortunately, sometimes we get so wrapped up in maintaining the house that we forget to take time to encourage those who live in it.

A marriage counselor I know used to talk about the "language of love." He said that men communicate their love by working hard, bringing home a paycheck, and simply coming home every night. They often forget to communicate. Women often also neglect to communicate, and yet we still hold the expectation that our husbands should *know* that we love them.

For this dilemma, we can seek the wisdom of Matthew 7:12: "Whatever you want men to do to you, do also to them." We like to be told we are loved and appreciated; therefore we need to tell our spouses how much we love and appreciate them. Actions do not always speak louder than words. Words matched with action speak volumes!

When my older son, Char, was getting married, he asked me for my best advice. I gave it to him. "Char, from the day I married your dad until this very day, he has told me two things. Every day he has told me that he loves me and that I am beautiful. Not that I believe that latter, but I believe *he* does, and that's good enough for me."

It's true. If ever I have entertained a thought of giving up on my marriage, the constant reminder of Brian's love and affection toward me has given me more than pause. Where else am I going to find that unwavering devotion and delusion (thinking I am beautiful)? It has also brought me so much security—something women crave in a relationship.

My son has been happily married over three years now. Recently, we had the opportunity to visit a garden together. In a moment alone I asked him if he had followed my advice. "Every day!" he responded. That's my boy!

Men want to be adored. Often work is the place where they receive the most satisfaction. When they come home, the wife is ready and waiting with the long honey-do list and notations of where they didn't measure up the last time. Is it any wonder then that many men prefer work to home?

I had a friend who constantly complained about her husband. He was a great father, super-attentive to her needs, and good-looking. As an addendum to her complaints she would say, "But we will never get divorced." One day I simply tired of her carping. In no uncertain terms I told her that whether she realized it or not she was on the short road to divorce. She looked at me with alarm.

"Listen!" I said. "Your husband is good-looking. He has a great personality. He makes good money. There are a hundred women that would go after him in a second if they knew that he wasn't appreciated at home. If you keep at him like this, it's just a matter of time until he begins to succumb to their charms."

About two hours later she called my house to tell me how much she loved and appreciated her husband. She told me they were never going to get a divorce because she realized how extremely blessed she was to have an attentive husband, a great father to her kids, and a faithful man to boot.

I'm not always so blunt, but all of us need a wake-up call at one point or another. I knew a woman who had aspirations for another man in the fellowship. She kicked her husband out because of this, but the relationship she fantasized over never materialized. In the meantime, some other woman realized that a great guy had just been forsaken and snatched him up!

Can I be honest with you? While we might enjoy the skillfully penned tales of Jane Austen, such as *Pride and Prejudice*, women need to remember that Mr. Darcy doesn't exist. He is the figment of a spinster's mind. Nonetheless, women spend their time waiting for men who stare at them from across the room, always smell like musk and wood, and whisper an endless stream of romantic sentiments. If we dwell on the charms of a fantasy, we will miss the wonderful, simple-hearted man who goes to work every day and comes home faithfully.

Simply Be Thankful

When your daily routine and the demands at hand cause thanksgiving for your husband to fade from your heart, it is great to remember all the things you loved about him when you impatiently waited to join him in marriage. Think about the things that drew you to him in the first place. Perhaps you might want to write them down and remind him of those things that you treasure in him.

I have found that when I thank Brian for doing the dishes I usually get a clean kitchen for a good week. I have learned that an acknowledgment and thank-you can get me a lot of mileage in my marriage.

Recently, I was praying with a friend. Her husband is going through a tough battle. He is standing up for truth and getting quite a bit of flak for his integrity. As she prayed, she began to cry. She was thanking God for the privilege of being married to him. It blessed me to hear her thank God for her husband's leadership and upright character.

Express your gratitude to God and to your husband. You will find that your spirit of thanksgiving returns with an enduring brightness.

Focused Attention

I have a terrible habit of zoning out. There are times when Brian is pouring out his heart to me, and I'll realize partway through the conversation that I have not paid attention to what he is saying. I've missed the chance to give him the gift of my undivided, loving attention.

Can you relate to a multitasking mind? Do you ever find yourself doing one thing while thinking what seems to be five separate thoughts? I can be looking at someone and appearing to listen and at the same time be thinking about how I am going to piece a quilt together or fix a broken lamp at home. I have to order myself to listen and concentrate. Brian has been on the receiving end of my wandering mind on more than one occasion.

When our husbands talk, they need our full attention. Consider how lucky you are if you have a spouse who does want to share about his life and his day. Or who respects your opinion enough to present you with his concerns or upcoming decisions. Do not take phone calls when your husband wants to talk. And don't start doing housework or going through the mail as he presents what's on his mind. Stop what you are doing and turn your eyes and heart and mind toward him. He will feel loved and adored when you make this effort to truly hear him.

Make sure he knows that the attention he needs is always available to him from you, his wife. This will prevent him from looking elsewhere when he needs to talk.

Marriage is an investment. The more we put into it, the more we will get out of it. We need to invest ourselves, our time, our emotions, our love, and our energy in our marriage. In time, our investment will yield great dividends.

A WORD TO THE MEN:

Christ Is Your Role Model

B Guys, God's Word is pretty simple and straightforward: "Husbands, love your wives as Christ loved the church and gave Himself for her." Love is the wellspring from which everything else will flow. Do you want to know how to encourage your marriage, how to secure your marriage, how to assure you have a good marriage? Four words: Husbands, love your wives!

How do we do that practically? By following the example of Jesus.

Loving as Christ Loved

I've sat in counseling appointments many times and listened to married couples squabble and bicker, threatening one another with separation or divorce. My head is full of knowledge about what they ought to be doing, but as they argue and talk over one another, I find myself saying, "Your problems are not due to a lack of information, but rather to a lack of application, and until you're ready to start doing what the Bible says to do I can't help you." When Paul calls men to follow the example of Christ in loving their wives as He loved the church, he is communicating two things there that I want to highlight.

Encouragement Through Cherishing

First he tells us that we are to *cherish* our wives. While this word is not common in our everyday conversations, we can put it into action by holding our wives dear and lovingly caring for them. In cherishing our wives we will see them as precious, and in turn we will act compassionately and sensitively toward them.

I have had to learn to become sensitive to Cheryl's needs. If I'm not intentional about following God's commands, I am the "bull in the china shop," trampling on my wife's feelings. Once she was trying to express to me how exhausted and overwhelmed she'd become by all the cooking, cleaning, and entertaining she was doing because of the steady stream of visitors I invited to stay with us on their way through London. I never stopped to think that while I was showing guests around the city or chatting over coffee, she was at home doing all the hard work! So when she expressed her weariness to me, longing for a little sympathy and help, I came back with something like, "You need to quit feeling sorry for yourself and just be a servant!"

Those were probably the cruelest words I'd ever spoken to her (though at the time I didn't realize that), and understandably, she lost it. We yelled and bickered for several hours until God finally got it through my thick head that I had brought all of this strife on myself because of my failure to love my wife and cherish her as Christ did the church.

What a lesson that was for me in the need to be sensitive to my wife's emotional needs! Had I demonstrated the kind of love toward Cheryl that Christ exemplified for me, I would have said something like, "Sweetheart, you have been working so hard, and I'm so thankful for the sacrificial love you constantly show me, the kids, and our guests. Why don't you relax a bit and let me do that for you?" She would've felt cherished and supported. And chances are, my empathy would've helped ease her weariness and renew her strength to serve.

Look for ways to cherish your wife this week. Listen to her and look beyond your motivations or needs so you can understand how circumstances impact her.

Encouragement Through Serving

Paul provides us with an important second illustration to follow. He says that Christ loved the church and gave Himself for her. Men, the love that we are to have toward our wives is a sacrificial love, a love that is demonstrated in our laying down our lives for our wives. I doubt that most of us would ever have the opportunity to literally lay down our lives for our wives, but there are many ways we can lay down our lives daily for them by dying to ourselves, dying to our own will and desires, and living to bless them. This happens when we do as Jesus did. He did not come to be served, but to serve and to give His life.

The example we have in Jesus is in great contrast to the model the world presents...the man's world. Now, things have changed considerably in our culture for women, but there still exists the perspective that married life, home life, and family life revolve around the man. He is the king of his castle, as it's said—and many Christian men have either bought into or inherited from their fathers that mentality. That's the model that has been passed down, not through the teaching and example of Jesus Christ and the apostles, but through the traditions of fallen, sinful, selfish men.

Christianity Is Radical

Now, there are plenty of folks in the mainstream culture who want to blame Christianity for the historical oppression of women and the whole idea of male dominance we are talking about here. But the facts are quite different. As a matter of fact, it was the teaching of the New Testament that really revolutionized the world in this particular area. The New Testament teaching flew right in the face of the views that were held at the time. Let's take a brief look at this issue by considering a few examples.

During biblical times, the rabbis believed that women were simply servants. In fact, they taught the men to pray like this: "God, I thank you that I am not a Gentile, a slave, or a woman, amen." They also said things like, "He who talks with a woman in public brings evil upon himself." "One is not so much to greet a woman publicly." "Let the words of the law be burned, rather than committed to a woman." "If a man teaches his daughter the law, it is as though he taught her lechery."*

It's important to understand that the rabbis' teaching was a distortion or a perversion of what the Old Testament itself actually said. The contention that Jesus had with the leaders of His day was not so much over what Moses did or didn't say. Rather, it was their misinterpretation and misapplication of what the Scriptures said that brought Jesus into conflict with them.

This attitude toward women existed not only among the ancient Jews; the Greeks had a very similar perspective. The attitude toward women among the Athenians and the Spartans was appalling. One Athenian orator and statesman said, "We have courtesans [high-class prostitutes] for the sake of pleasure. We have concubines for the sake of daily cohabitation, and we have wives for the purpose of having children legitimately and being faithful guardians for our household affairs."†

What's interesting to me is that so many of the humanistic

---

* Alvin J. Schmidt, *How Christianity Changed the World* (Grand Rapids, MI: Zondervan, 2004), 97-102.
† Schmidt, 97-102.

thinkers of today want to trace our cultural lineage back to Greece rather than to Judeo-Christian influences. They conveniently overlook the oppression of women in Greek society. In Roman culture a woman was essentially the slave of a man's lower passions. According to Roman law a man had absolute power over his wife and all her possessions. He could divorce her at any time for any offense whatsoever. He had full authority to chastise his wife and in some cases even to kill her. To kill his wife for a nonadulterous offense, the husband ordinarily required the consent of an extended family tribunal; but in the case of adultery no such consent was necessary.*

Similar perspectives on women are still prevalent today in Islamic, Hindu, Buddhist, animist, and even atheistic cultures. So modern anthropologists and sociologists who blame Christianity for the oppression of women are either ignorant of the facts, or they are guilty of historical revisionism.

Serving by Giving Ourselves

All these cultural attitudes underlie the notion we talked about, that of being the king of our castle. But that's not the Christian's model. Our model is Christ, the servant of all, the one who gave Himself completely to those He loved.

Years ago, a young couple that I was going to marry asked if I could write some vows that would be more biblically based than the traditional ones. I did, and ever since then those vows have replaced the traditional ones for every Christian couple whose ceremony I have performed. In them, the man at one point says, "I promise to serve you as Christ serves the church, and to give myself for you as Jesus gave Himself for me."

In accord with the words of the husband's vow above, giving of ourselves, our time, our attention, and our wills for the sake of our wives is a loving, godly way to encourage our marriages.

---

* Schmidt, 97-102.

How do I do this for Cheryl? Here's a quick list that might help as you shape your own path of encouragement:

1. Instead of insisting on doing what I want to do (which I did for many years), I let her decide what we'll do on my day off, or where we'll go to dinner, or where we'll stay on vacation, and so on.

2. After Cheryl's made a wonderful meal, I tell her to go enjoy some time alone and let me take care of the dishes.

3. I'm not naturally inclined toward household maintenance, but because I know Cheryl is blessed by such efforts, I fix the plumbing, put up a shelf, or tend to the yard.

These seemingly small gestures go a long way to show your wife you love her and to make her feel secure in the marriage relationship.

Encouragement Through Kindness

Finally, we can greatly encourage our wives and ultimately our marriages through simply speaking kindly and lovingly to them. My wife responds to praise and, honestly, I love giving it to her. She's worthy of all I can give and more.

For as long as I can remember I have told her every day that I love her and that she's beautiful. I know that she doesn't always feel lovable or beautiful, but I can always sense her being encouraged when I tell her that. I like to tell her how good her cooking is; I like to tell her how thankful I am for her; I tell her how glad I am that she is the mother of my children; I tell her how blessed I am by her love and support and prayers for me. And of course I tell her all of this because I mean it. This isn't a formula I've come up with so I can have a happy marriage—it's what is in my heart toward her.

Now don't get me wrong. I am not a "hopeless romantic" who

wanders about expressing loving sentiments toward my wife every minute of every day. But as you've probably heard, love is not a feeling, it is a choice. I have chosen to do this, and through His grace God has filled my heart more and more with love for Cheryl. And He'll do the same for any man who will make that choice.

Men, choose to encourage your wife by learning to cherish her, give yourself in loving service to her, and tell her how much you love and appreciate her. This is what it means to encourage your marriage.

Build Up, Lift Up

Growing together in a godly way means that you draw closer to one another. It means that you redirect your focus from the desert of the material world, upward to the wealth and fruitfulness of heavenly purposes. Keeping your eyes and your heart on God's best for your marriage is the right way to keep your priorities in line with God's will.

As you look up for the wisdom, guidance, and grace you need to get through each day, you will be reminded to build up and lift up your loved one. You accomplish this through kindness of speech, generosity with time and attention, and actions that show support and unconditional love.

And most importantly, lift up your wife, lift up your husband, in prayer. When you give their needs and concerns to God, His care and lasting love will inspire your spouse in remarkable ways.

KNOWING IS GROWING

1. Sit down together and express your love and gratitude for one another. The simple declaration "I love you" means so much.

2. Discuss the feelings you had when you first fell in love with each other. Describe what you saw and loved in one another at

that time. It's always enjoyable to go back in time and recount the first time you saw one another, your first conversation, your first date, the first time you held hands, and so on. How are your perspectives on the stories different?

3. Plan a day this month to write letters to one another expressing your love and restating your vows or reinforcing how you want to grow together from this point on. Letters are very romantic and can be cherished for years to come.

GROWING-TOGETHER GRACE

Father, You are our endless source of encouragement and hope. Give us hearts and minds that turn toward Your goodness so we may gather it and share it with each other. Renew in us a daily desire to serve You and our marriage with deep devotion. When we struggle to submit, remind us of Your sacrifice so that we might serve each other with glad hearts. Bless our marriage, Lord. And may our marriage be a blessing to You.

Essential
FIVE:

Exemplify

Speak the things which are proper for sound doctrine: that the older men be sober, reverent, temperate, sound in faith, in love, in patience; the older women likewise, that they be reverent in behavior, not slanderers, not given to much wine, teachers of good things—that they admonish the young women to love their husbands, to love their children, to be discreet, chaste, homemakers, good, obedient to their own husbands, that the word of God may not be blasphemed.

TITUS 2:1-5

Exemplify

The little storefront church was crowded with young people. Their exuberance energized the room. With great anticipation, the group waited for the young man up front, our son, to break open his Bible.

"Turn in your Bibles to 1 Corinthians 11. We will be studying verses 1 through 10 tonight." Brian and I practically groaned. We knew how difficult that particular passage was to expound on. It was a controversial chapter for many pastors, yet our 27-year-old son, Char, was about to teach his burgeoning congregation from this knotty text.

Silently we prayed. He read the first ten verses that begin with Paul appealing to the Corinthians to imitate him even as he imitated Christ. From there the text covered the roles of men and women in the church. Paul talked to those in the Corinthian culture about head coverings for women.

In the contemporary church, debate often centers on this verse because believers don't know what to do with the idea of head coverings. Is this a biblical mandate for women? Is it about making women lesser than men? It brings confusion to present-day Christians. We continued to watch our son with great respect. He had not chosen an easy message to share, and yet he seemed eager to dig in and bring out the truth of the Scripture.

Char sighed as he finished reading verses 1 through 10, and then he plunged into his message. He took verse 10 first. "For this reason the woman ought to have a symbol of authority on her head, because of the angels." He explained that God created men to be men and women to be women. In the scheme of God's creation, He had a divine purpose and role for each sex. When women act like women and fulfill their God-given positions, and men behave like men, thus fulfilling their God-given roles, God is glorified before the angels of heaven, he taught.

Char believed that Paul used the specific example of head coverings because, in the church of Corinth, they were used by women only. It was a culturally relevant illustration, he continued, for Paul to use to illuminate femininity in the church of Corinth. It gave them a tangible, practical way to understand Paul's message of honoring God as men and women.

As a proud mother and father, we listened with rapt attention, stealing a moment here and there to smile at each other during our son's sermon. Each smile communicated our unspoken message to each other: "He got it right. Our son really got it right!"

God-Given Roles

As cultures and societal practices change, the roles of men and women are constantly being redefined. Yet the principles of God's purpose in creating men and women as separate and unique creations from each other have not.

Presently, the atmosphere permeating Hollywood, the fashion industry, and other influencers in society is a blending of male and female so that there is little distinction left. It is in vogue for men to act like women and women to act like men. But this is not how God created things to be. The church is to be a place where the glory, purpose, and design of God in creating women to be women and men to be men are seen.

Women are to embrace their femininity. They are to be tender, gentle, and reveal their strength as helpmates. Men are to be strong, protective leaders. Both sexes are to dress appropriately. The looks of femininity and masculinity might change in outward appearance (men don't wear long robes or togas publicly anymore), but the distinction designed by God remains the same.

It was God who created Adam as a man. It was God who fashioned Adam from the dust of the earth. It was God who said, "It is not good that a man should be alone, I will make him a helper comparable to him."

Notice that God did not decide to make a helper just like Adam. God created a helper who would be complementary to him. God created Eve differently than and separately from Adam and for different purposes. It's truly a wonderful gift that God didn't want these intended partners to be identical. Think of how much trouble our marriages would be in if we were the same!

The idea of men and women being created for different purposes may fly in the face of the egalitarian spirit of this age, but it is God's purpose in creation and for healthy marriages. It is also our great gift as married couples! After God created these two distinct but complementary beings, He pronounced a blessing on their unity. We too are blessed in our marriages when we follow God's purposes for us as men, as women, as partners.

In his short epistle to Titus, Paul assigns his younger co-worker the task of teaching the men and women their God-given roles in the church.

> Speak the things which are proper for sound doctrine: that the older men be sober, reverent, temperate, sound in faith, in love, in patience; the older women likewise, that they be reverent in behavior, not slanderers, not given to much wine, teachers of good things—that they admonish the young women to love their husbands, to love their children, to be discreet, chaste, homemakers, good, obedient to their own husbands, that the word of God may not be blasphemed (Titus 2:1-5).

Notice the distinguishing characteristics of the older men and the older women. Both are to be reverent or respectful, but there is a definite difference between the behaviors that are required.

Some men feel that part of their masculinity is to handle the finances. Other men relinquish this role to the women as the keepers of the home, so they can do the business of providing for the family without distraction. Finances are not the true test of masculinity. The hallmark of masculinity is standing in Christ against the forces of the world, the flesh, and the devil. Masculinity comes as a man receives his marching orders from the Captain of his salvation, the Lord Jesus Christ.

While some women are stay-at-home moms, others work outside the home and help to supplement the household income. Neither working outside the home nor in the home is the mark of femininity. Femininity is defined by the greater principle of allowing God to work in you the purposes for which you were created.

How to Exemplify Our Roles at Home

B Contrary to how some view the division of the sexes, masculinity and femininity are not predicated on who cleans the house, does the dishes, or cooks the food. Masculinity is the leadership role the man takes in the household as he stands before God on behalf of the spiritual, physical, and emotional well-being of his home. Femininity is the role of a woman as a spiritual and emotional support to the leadership of her husband. The role of support might be even to fill in the deficits her husband leaves.

Men are great at forgetting or omitting important steps. When we lived in England, I would often announce a fellowship meal the following Sunday for the congregants. I would always assure Cheryl that she didn't have to worry—I would take care of everything. But Cheryl did have cause for concern. Things like napkins or serviettes (a British word for napkins), tableware, and cups for drinking never entered my mind. My focus was on the food and fellowship. Rather than pointing out all that was needed to make these times of fellowship happen smoothly, Cheryl would gather some women together and they would facilitate the meal with all the necessary accessories. The fellowship meals were always a success!

Years ago we had a couple from Eastern Europe stay with us for an extended time. That man watched how Cheryl and I interacted and scrutinized my participation in housework around our home. One day he approached me as I was doing the dishes. "In my culture men never do the dishes," he said with an air of disdain.

"There is a greater culture that I answer to," I replied. "I am a servant of Jesus Christ, and His culture instructs those who are the greatest in the household to be servants. I am choosing to show Cheryl my love and appreciation for all she does for me, our children, our home, and in the church by doing the dishes for her."

The man dropped his head. "I do the shopping for my wife," he said, trying to justify his omissions.

I laughed. "I think that is the part Cheryl enjoys doing the most."

Later, as he was preparing to return to his country, the man said to me, "You have given me a lot to ponder about being the servant in my own house."

What are you modeling to your family and to those who observe your family in action? Do they notice the small acts of kindness that you offer one another? Are they able to see how you both enjoy your God-given strengths?

Each time you welcome someone into your home, each time you serve others as a family, and each time you are enhancing your marriage by living out your purpose, you are honoring God in your roles as man and wife.

Curse or Blessing?

C I grew up in the proverbial fishbowl. As the daughter of a well-known and well-loved pastor and his equally loved wife, I was always being watched. Frequently I was approached by someone who would say, "I saw you the other day and you were doing…" or, "Is that attire appropriate for church?" Usually they were referring to the flip-flops I loved to wear with nearly everything.

Pretty quickly, I realized that being watched was either a curse or a blessing depending on how I chose to live my life. If I dedicated my life fully to Jesus it could prove to be an opportunity to show others how to live for Him. If I chose to live my life for my own fulfillment, it would be a curse. I would be caught, chastised, reported on, and rebuked at every corner. In viewing both alternatives, I chose to live for Jesus.

In the same way, how you choose to live in your marriage can either be a blessing or a curse. If you as a couple choose to find and obey your God-ordained roles in the marriage, your marriage will be an example and blessing to others. However, should you choose to seek your own fulfillment without regard to the will of God or the feelings of your spouse, your marriage will be a curse to you and a stumbling block to others.

Brian and I once conversed with a young man who was very liberal in his theology. He told us that he had come to his conclusions because his parents, who both claimed to be godly Christians, could never get along. Isn't that telling? He had not predicated his philosophies on biblical truths, but on his parents' unhappy marriage.

A godly marriage presents the opportunity to showcase the original intent, purpose, and glory of God in the creation of male and female. It also sets a pattern for others who want to have godly marriages. Your relationship has the potential to not only be a blessing to you and your spouse but also help others who desire to have a blessed marriage.

A good marriage is a blessing to others. A bad one is a curse to those in it, those around it, those born into it, and those observing it. When others see a bad marriage they get fearful about entering into such a covenant with another. They lose faith in the power of God to heal, work through, and bless marriage.

The Power of a Godly Marriage

People are attracted to success, happiness, and wholeness. And when they see something that works well, they want to copy it. If you try someone's spaghetti and it is the best pasta you've ever had—you want the recipe. You want to know how you can prepare the same dish with the same rewarding results. When people witness someone living out faith and purpose, they are attracted to such a life of fulfillment. They will soon want to know the secret to such a good life.

This is the power of a godly marriage. When we live out God's best for our relationships and strive to serve and honor Him, people notice the resulting quality of life. Whether you realize it or not, people are observing your marriage. They are taking mental notes. Maybe it is a stranger at a café paying attention to how you and your spouse are enjoying each other's company. Maybe it is someone you know who unwittingly sees you having an argument. It is up to you whether your marriage is providing an example of good and righteous fruit to your family and to those you meet. Just as people want the formula for a successful business or the secret ingredient for the best cookies, they'll want to know what goes into a godly marriage. Some may even take the time to get the directions.

But keep in mind that a lot of people, men especially, will want to bypass directions and get to the results. They'll look at the picture in the cookbook of the final entrée and say, "That's what I want" even when they are reluctant to read the list of ingredients and instructions. The same is true in marriage. Though many couples won't take the time to read a book on marriage, they *will* notice the picture of a happily married couple and say, "That's what I want." And from there, they will listen and watch and hopefully imitate the godly practices.

A godly marriage glorifies God. When the man loves his wife and the woman respects and submits to her husband as unto the Lord, the divine purposes of God are seen.

I know a husband and wife who are as poor as church mice—however, they are rich in love and mutual respect for each other. This respect and love is the hallmark of their lives, and it is irresistible. Their daughter longs to one day have a marriage just like her parents', apart from any consideration of financial security.

A godly marriage gives hope to a struggling one. It makes a statement that is louder than any sermon. It shouts that marriage is worth it! It promises emotional and spiritual rewards to anyone who will amend their attitudes and seek God's blessing in their own marriage.

Who Is Watching Your Marriage?

B We're all being observed whether we know it or not. No, I am not referring to "Big Brother," but to different audiences that are taking note. The world is watching our marriages. That's right—nonbelievers are watching them. I cannot tell you the number of people who tell me they plan on "getting religious" after they are married. Why is that? Because they have noted that marriages that put God first are happiest and most successful. Of course, I encourage them to let God do the leading right now so that they enter marriage spiritually prepared for its demands and rewards.

In one of Cheryl's exercise classes the women were complaining about their spouses. My wife piped up, "I am really sorry to hear about your marriages. I got a great man the first time off."

A woman looked at her quizzically and in a rich Scottish accent asked her, "And what makes your man so special?"

Cheryl thought for a moment, and not wanting to put anyone off she answered, "He's kind and godly."

"Yes. Those are the best characteristics that a man can have," the woman answered somberly.

Many times in that same class the women asked Cheryl questions about our marriage and what made it work. She got the opportunity to share with the class members about the power of God working through our lives and the promise of God to work in the lives of anyone who would give Him the opportunity to do so.

Cheryl and I love to get coffee at a certain place in the city where we live. Whenever I get a cup of coffee without Cheryl the employees there always ask me where she is. They have grown accustomed to seeing us together.

One of the younger women there commented to me how she was so encouraged to see the way Cheryl and I seem to have so much fun together. "I see you sitting and talking to each other and laughing." When I told her that it had been that way for 31 years she was amazed. She inquired about our success and I had the opportunity to share with her about the power of God working in our lives to bless our marriage.

Our kids also are watching our marriages more closely than we realize. Our own children have observed our marriage firsthand. They have seen Cheryl and me argue intensely. They have seen us negotiate. They have seen us reconcile. They have seen us pray together. They have seen us cry with each other. They have seen us laugh. They have seen us work together as a team, and they have seen us work separately, oceans apart, as a team. They have seen us resist temptation and turn away from flirtation.

When our older son was four, he took upon himself the job of safeguarding my marriage to his mother. One day as Cheryl was buying paint at a paint store, Char felt that the balding attendant was a little too friendly with his mom. Placing his hands on his tiny hips, and with a lisp no one could miss, he looked right at the man and announced, "She's married, you know—to my dad!"

Even at four years old, the union of his parents was of the utmost importance to our son. He was watching even then.

There is a greater audience, though, than the church, the world, and even our children. According to 1 Corinthians 11:10, Ephesians 3:10, and 1 Peter 1:12, invisible principalities and powers are watching. That's right. Our marriages are being observed by unseen powers. They are scrutinizing God's creation of male and female and of marriage in order to glorify Him, or in order to dishonor Him and His creation. A godly marriage showcases His power and purposes to angelic deities.

Your marriage has the potential to highlight the power of God to impressionable couples in your church, to the world that is watching, to your children who are wondering, and to the principalities that are waiting to see if God is truly wise in His purposes. And He is ready to supply you with all you need to have a godly and God-glorifying marriage.

What Does a Godly Marriage Exemplify?

Many godly characteristics can be best seen—or only seen—in

marriage. It is one of the greatest environments in which the fruit of the Spirit can be exemplified and proven. Think about it. Marriage unites two completely diverse and unique individuals with fragile and broken human natures, moving them beyond what is naturally possible into a wholesome, fulfilling, gracious unity! Only God can accomplish something like that.

Marriage exemplifies a love that can endure. Most relationships between men and women fail at some point or other because they don't have or don't depend on the divine mortar of God to keep them together. When people find out how long Cheryl and I have been married they often gasp and ask, "How have you been able to keep the relationship together so long?" I answer that I haven't kept it together, but God has.

When I first took those vows to love and to cherish in sickness and in health, I really wasn't aware of what I was saying. I just wanted to get through the ceremony and on with life. I never realized the intention of those promises until I was struck down with chronic fatigue syndrome. Cheryl was pregnant at the time with our second child.

As I lay in bed I knew that this scenario was not what she had signed up for. Yet she stayed with me to nurse me back to health. She drove me back and forth to the doctor and prayed fervently for my recovery. In time I was able to resume some aspects of my former schedule, but it took a long time for the chronic fatigue to ebb enough for me to take back all my responsibilities.

There were people observing us during this time. They saw Cheryl's fidelity and love for me in my sickness, and they were encouraged and helped by her example. I have often shared this with others when I am counseling or teaching.

For her part, Cheryl would talk about my perseverance with her through four pregnancies and the accompanying range of emotions and shapes her body took. There are times when I compliment her and she retorts, "I thank God for deluding your mind to think I am beautiful."

There is no atmosphere that can exemplify the glory of grace in the same way as marriage. Grace has often been defined as "God's riches at Christ's expense." But it is even more than that. Grace forgives our sins, overlooks our shortcomings, brings us into the very family of God, and lavishes us with undeserved blessings. Grace also supplies us with the power to obey the commands of Jesus.

The same grace from God is exemplified in marriage when we, by His power, choose to forgive our spouses, overlook their shortcomings, restore a heart-to-heart relationship with them, and lavish undeserved blessings upon them. Grace is God's divine power working in us so we might obey and follow His directives in our marriage and our lives. This divine grace is beautifully displayed in a godly marriage.

Such a marriage affords the opportunity for faith to be observed. As a couple together prays, believes, and holds on to the promises of God for their marriage, family, finances, and livelihood, the reward of faith is evidenced.

Faith and Love in Action

A couple we know went through some extreme financial setbacks. The husband was laid off for over two years. During that time, they continued to seek God for their family, well-being, and finances. For over two years He miraculously paid every bill and sustained them. After two years the company hired him back. Whenever another couple was struggling with financial hardships we would recommend that they meet and have dinner with these friends. Over dinner, our friends, usually holding hands, would testify to the keeping and supplying power of God they witnessed for over two years. What an inspiration and example they were and are to the power of faith in a marriage!

Marriage exemplifies so many unique and wonderful attributes. A godly marriage can exhibit unity, endurance, fulfillment, joy, and happiness. It can provide security, promise, and a sense of belonging. And most importantly, it exemplifies the blessing of God. He desires to bless His institution—marriage. He wants to use your marriage to showcase His perfection and wisdom in creating men and women as distinct beings with ordained purposes.

God's ultimate purpose in creating marriage was and is to *bless*. He chose marriage as the institution by which He would bless men and women. Proverbs 18:22 states, "He who finds a wife finds a good thing; and obtains favor from the LORD."

God is ready and waiting to bless your marriage. His desire is to make your marriage an example that others can emulate. Through your marriage, He desires to showcase the fruit of the Spirit and the power of His Spirit at work in the lives of two frail and fault-ridden human beings. Won't you let Him make your marriage a showcase for blessing? He will give you the power to do so if you only ask Him to and surrender to His will and directives.

KNOWING IS GROWING

1. Have you relinquished your distinct roles and purposes as a man and a woman in order to fulfill societal expectations or to please other people? Discuss how you can each embrace the qualities God has appointed to you. How will celebrating those purposes and differences enhance your marriage? See it as an exciting adventure to grow together as husband and wife.

2. Spend a date night or a relaxing evening on the front porch and talk about the models of marriage you both have had. Good ones. Bad ones. How did those examples shape your convictions for your marriage today? Create a list of three godly attributes you both really want to work on in your marriage.

    1.

    2.

    3.

3. Consider arranging a get-together with a couple you respect and admire. Talk to them about what makes their marriage so strong. Your interest in their commitment to God's purpose for marriage will encourage them and will reinforce what you want your marriage to become.

4. Now think of a couple you know who is struggling or even a newlywed couple who is starting to find their way around in the land of matrimony. What can you both do to encourage this couple? Commit to praying for them and for a way to inspire them. Have them over for a barbecue. Consider starting a Bible study or a dessert and discussion group for couples. See where and how God leads you to exemplify the holy union of marriage.

GROWING-TOGETHER GRACE

Our Creator, You made us, man and woman, to have unique strengths and abilities and inclinations. Sharpen our understanding of these attributes. May we seek Your Word regularly so we walk, live, and love in line with Your will. Give us hearts that long for godliness. Lead us to a couple who present a living example of Your vision for marriage. And let us become willing mentors to others. Keep us authentic as we show our weaknesses as well as our strengths so we can point to Your grace as the tie that binds, the love that nurtures, and the miracle that causes us to grow together. Amen.

Essential SIX:

Empathize

Let us consider one another in order
to stir up love and good works.

HEBREWS 10:24

Empathize

Many marriages falter because one person or the other forgets the essentiality of empathizing with their spouse. In Romans 12:15-16, Paul the apostle highlighted this essential when he instructed, "Rejoice with those who rejoice, and weep with those who weep. Be of the same mind toward one another."

Empathy is the practice of thinking about and trying to feel what another person is feeling.

Too many spouses get self-absorbed and self-centered. They cannot for a moment take time to consider the feelings of their partner. They focus only on how they feel and how they are emotionally affected. When empathy is omitted from a marriage, you end up with two people who do not understand each other and who might even resent one another over time.

God calls us to see beyond our needs and our wants so we can understand and serve our spouse. Developing the essential of empathy will strengthen your union and your connection. It will become a foundation for more meaningful conversations, sincere pursuits of common dreams, and the fulfillment of God's purposes for your marriage. And it all starts with the heart.

The Heart Connection of Empathy

The moment could have changed the course of my marriage forever. I felt her warm hand on mine. She was an old friend and nothing could have seemed more natural in the picturesque setting.

It had been an emotionally charged evangelistic outreach to small villages nestled beyond the Iron Curtain. The youth in the villages had responded enthusiastically to our traveling ensemble and the message of the gospel. All of us, three guys and two girls, had been riding high on what God had done. We had left our families and church behind in order to work without any hindrances. Cheryl was at home overseeing the welfare of our children, home, and even our beloved dog while I traveled to foreign lands. I had teasingly called her the "keeper of the stuff," in reference to a passage in 1 Samuel where David declares that the one who "tarrieth [stays] by the stuff" shall share equally with the one who "goeth down to battle."

Our small traveling group of missionaries had bonded together in a spiritual way. Together we had endured the hardships of going without familiar foods, trying to communicate with limited language skills, moving from place to place, and staying in somewhat primitive accommodations. We had also formed a makeshift band, and the joy of harmonizing instruments and voices together had knit our hearts together. But our camaraderie deepened most of all as we experienced the wonder of seeing new believers coming to Christ. We shared in the elation of being eyewitnesses of the extraordinary things God had done.

So when I felt the gentle pressure of a hand resting against my own, I almost didn't notice. I glanced to my left. The woman smiled innocently at me. Suddenly, a pang hit my heart and a voice shouted in my mind, *How would Cheryl feel about this young woman holding your hand?* It might only be an innocent gesture, but I had left a trusting wife at home. She believed in my fidelity. She believed in my love. She had released me to do the Lord's service. The thought of her being hurt by another woman holding my hand was not a good thought.

I subtly pulled my hand away and gave the young woman a look that sent a clear message that I was not interested in going there.

I didn't think my actions were observed by anyone at the time.

However, when I got home, Cheryl questioned me about the trip. I shared with her all the exciting things God had done. I shared with her about the people we had met and the way they responded to the Word of God. She listened intently. "Anything else?" she asked.

I sighed deeply. "Yeah," I answered. "I thought about you a lot." I knew that my wife felt emotionally distanced from me because she had not been a participant in the trip. The women on the trip seemed to now have a connection with me that she did not have. This bothered Cheryl.

So I went on to tell her about the incident. She smiled and said she already knew but just needed to hear it from me.

I explained to Cheryl how the Lord had prompted my heart at that moment to think of her and how she would feel if I'd even entertained a thought of someone else. I told her how I would never want to hurt her. There was a special connection to her even when I was in another land, because I knew she was at home being a faithful wife. I knew my heart was completely safe with her, and I wanted her to feel the same safety with my heart.

As I said, this moment could have changed my marriage forever. And in the end, it did change my marriage. Because of empathy... because of the heart connection Cheryl and I had even across the miles, we felt closer than ever before. We were both learning to empathize with the other. My wife was thinking of me, far away in a foreign country sharing the gospel. Each morning and evening she would pray for me, anticipating what my day might bring and what needs would arise.

I was also thinking of her at home alone with the kids. I was praying for her as she took on my responsibilities as well as her own. We were both thinking tenderly of the heart that trusted the other heart so far away.

Awakening to Empathy

C I remember a particular incident years ago when I asked Brian a harmless question, and he answered in an unexpectedly cold way. I was so upset by his uncharacteristically rude response that I stormed upstairs, leaving him sitting alone in a corner chair of the living room.

As I slammed the pillows around under the guise of making the bed, I complained to God about how much I was doing in the marriage without any reward. I told Him that I was the one who made the meals, cleaned the house, and washed the clothes. I kept the kids dressed, clean, decently behaved, and groomed. I taught Sunday school and typed the church bulletin. And Brian clearly didn't appreciate me, because if he did he wouldn't speak to me so sharply.

As my thoughts became as messy and tumbled about as the pillows, the Spirit of the Lord broke through to my heart with a gentle rebuke. In my tirade about my good works, I hadn't even considered what might have been behind Brian's curt answer to me.

I sat down on the rumpled bed and asked the Lord to speak to me. He did. He told me that my husband was wrestling with a big decision. He was agonizing over what to do.

I tiptoed softly down the stairs. Brian was still in the chair where I had left him an hour before. "Brian, are you okay?" I asked. He swiveled the chair around and I could see the concern on his face.

"I am just so confused," he confessed. "I don't want to plunge the church into debt, and yet we are busting at the seams. I hate seeing those kids sweating in the school buses we use for Sunday-school classrooms."

In my self-focus, I hadn't realized how responsible Brian felt for the welfare of the church that was outgrowing its home. I knelt beside the chair and we prayed together for the right decision and right facility for God's people. God supplied both.

It was empathy that allowed me to see beyond my own feelings and understand the issues Brian was wrestling with. Empathy bonded us together and allowed us to be on the same page.

The Meaning of Empathy

To empathize is to consider another's feelings or predicament and to share those feelings or that predicament emotionally. It is to think about what is another's best interest or welfare. Jesus referred to this attitude in Matthew 7:12, when He commanded, "Whatever you want men to do to you, do also to them, for this is the Law and the Prophets."

We don't empathize enough! We often move on impulse—and from a very self-centered place. After all, the entire secular attitude around us lends itself to self-centered thinking. There are slogans all around us that communicate, "If it feels good, just do it." Others announce, "You owe it to yourself." It's not a popular notion to think about others. In fact the whole idea of sacrifice is missing from the popular mind-set.

Empathy requires that thought and consideration take place before action. Before we act on impulse, the feelings of our spouse need to be considered. It is important to ask yourself the following questions:

- How would my spouse feel if they found out I did this?
- Would this action be healthy or beneficial to my spouse and my marriage?

Think how many flirtations, bad decisions, and bad investments would be avoided if we took the time to think about what our wives or husbands would think.

The Practice of Empathy

B Empathy comes naturally to some people, but for most of us it must be developed. The good news is we have the Holy Spirit to prompt us to empathize and give us the power to do so. Hebrews 10:24 spells out the practice of empathy: "Let us consider one another in order to stir up love and good works."

Empathy requires consideration of someone other than yourself. It requires thinking about someone else. It means you must think about their day, their responsibilities, their hardships, their weaknesses, and their emotions.

Empathy has two considerations. The first consideration is to *avoid hurting your loved one*. In order not to injure our spouse, we must consider the words we use, the way we speak, and the things we do. Obviously this requires God's intervention in our hearts to make us sensitive to the way we speak and act.

Years ago Cheryl complained to a friend about the way our teenager was addressing her. Her friend recalled having the same problem and revealed how she'd been so desperate to show her daughter what her behavior was like that she decided to tape her teen during an outburst. The mother then played back the tape, only to be embarrassed by her own tone of voice and words. She realized she had been a participant in her daughter's bad behavior and she asked God to work in her so she would talk graciously to her teenager. He did.

Sometimes we are so focused on how we are being addressed that we don't realize how we're talking to and even provoking our spouse. Do we perhaps need to record our next conflict so we can recognize our own culpability?

The second consideration of empathy is to *bless your spouse*. This means you have to know what your spouse likes. Buy your wife the flowers she loves just to let her know you were thinking about her. Surprise her with dinner at her favorite restaurant. Do the dishes because she made dinner. Volunteer to tuck the kids into bed and read them the Bible story. Give her a hug...

Move beyond the words he or she uses and try to understand what is going on in their heart. Are they insecure? Afraid? Discouraged? Sad? Disappointed? Lonely?

Women need to think about the temptations, competition, and oppression their husbands are up against all day. What hardships is your husband facing at work? If you had had a hard day and were exhausted emotionally, mentally, and physically what would you like to be greeted with when you got home? Some men require an hour of quietness when they come in from a hectic day at work. Other men need a hug and to be treated with appreciation and praise. What does your husband need?

A great way to start the practice of empathy is to have the other write you a list of things they would like you to pray for them about.

Wives, ask your husbands how and what you can pray for them while they are at work. Husbands, ask your wives what you can pray for them. When we begin to pray for each other, empathy naturally (or should we say, supernaturally?) arises.

Requirements and Rewards of Empathy

Empathy, as we stated before, will require consideration of your spouse's feelings, activities, and hardships. It will also require knowledge of what they are going through emotionally and physically. You will need to know what they are facing each day. It will require putting yourself in their shoes in order to sense what they are feeling.

Empathy will also require limiting your liberties at times for love's sake. Though you might feel the freedom to do something and know it means nothing to you, for the sake of your spouse's feelings you might need to stop that activity.

Recently our son and daughter-in-law got in an argument over a certain term my son was using. The term bothered our daughter-in-law's sensibilities and she told him so. He argued that there was nothing wrong with the term and he enjoyed employing the phrase. They went round and round on this issue. Finally, my daughter-in-law took a different approach. "You might feel that this term is fine, and maybe it is. But simply because you love me and know it bothers me, will you not use it?" This got to our son.

He thought about the term he was using. Was it worth it to say it when he knew it was bothering his precious wife? He stopped using the term simply for love's sake.

Practicing empathy and causing that part of ourselves to grow might require sacrifice at different times. It also will require that you go the extra mile. Empathy requires mental energy, emotional commitment, and personal sacrifice, but it is well worth it. Empathy will put a husband and wife on the same page. It will enhance their understanding and appreciation of each other as no other practice can. This understanding will yield patience with each other's inadequacies, indelicacies, and weaknesses. It will also produce a deep sense of communion, fellowship, and compatibility as each one thinks about and considers the other.

In considering one another's needs and feelings, we conceive and enrich an appreciation for our spouse's role, hardships, and hopes. Ask God to help you begin to consider your spouse as never before, so that you might stir up him or her to good works.

KNOWING IS GROWING

1. Read aloud Paul's great call to empathy: "Rejoice with those who rejoice, and weep with those who weep. Be of the same mind toward one another" (Romans 12:15-16). Memorize this verse and encourage one another to follow its commands.

   - *Rejoice with those who rejoice.* Find ways to celebrate with one another. Celebrate the accomplishments or strengths of your spouse. Make a special treat because they were honored at work or because they showed strength under pressure. Write a card acknowledging or congratulating them for what they did and letting them know you are sharing their joy.

   - *Weep with those who weep.* How can you come alongside your spouse and support them during a time of trial or sorrow? Consider praying over them or writing out a prayer for them. Take time to sit with your loved one and listen as they express their hurts. Also, allow the silence to be a comfort. If they weep, be there in prayerful presence with them.

   - *Be of the same mind toward one another.* Work on this important aspect of empathy within your marriage. Talk to each other about what gives you cause for joy and cause for sorrow. You might not realize the depths of what you each carry inside you emotionally and spiritually day to day. Be gentle with one another and practice compassion. As you share, also be thinking about how you can come alongside one another and support the needs of your loved one.

2. Spend this week and this month nurturing your heart connection with one another and with God. Commit to daily prayer for your spouse. Now that you have a deeper understanding of their needs, devote time daily to bringing those needs before the Lord. Ask for a discerning heart and mind so you can act, speak, and serve with empathy.

GROWING-TOGETHER GRACE

Dear Lord, give us spirits and hearts that expand with empathy. Show us the way of compassion as we bring each other's burdens to Your care. Let us rejoice with each other over the small and big moments of delight and look for reasons to celebrate each other. Guide us to have empathy for those in our midst. Move us away from self-serving behavior so we find great satisfaction in serving one another, You, and others, near and far. Bless our union, God. May our hearts remain tethered to Your own so we remain connected no matter the circumstance.

Essential SEVEN:
Enlighten

*The thief does not come except to steal, and to
kill, and to destroy. I have come that they may have
life, and that they may have it more abundantly.*

JOHN 10:10

Enlighten

Like everything else God made and loves, marriage is a target of Satan's hatred. He hates it and is working overtime to destroy it, especially Christian marriage. If the devil can take down a Christian couple he can do a lot of damage to the cause of Christ. Unbelieving acquaintances, friends, and family members look at Christians failing in their marriages and question the reality of the power of the gospel. Children whose Christian parents have split up are often stumbled to the point of not wanting anything to do with Christ. They reason that if Jesus couldn't keep their parents' marriage from falling apart then He probably can't do much for them either.

God created the family unit as the ideal place for nurturing the next generation in the faith, and for this reason Satan bends every effort toward destroying it, beginning with the marital relationship.

When we enlighten our ways and our days with the Word of God and His truth, Satan's deception has less chance to gain leverage in our lives. We can compare the thoughts, actions, behaviors, longings, urges, and areas of agitation to God's purpose and plan and know whether they are truly of Him or if they are incited by the enemy.

Let's enlighten our marriages by unveiling what we need to know about the forces of darkness and God's great gift of illumination for our individual paths and marital journeys.

Shedding Light on Spiritual Warfare

B In my early years of married life and ministry Cheryl and I experienced a recurring situation that was very frustrating to me. It seemed that every time I was about to engage in any ministry activity, especially teaching the Bible, we would have a confrontation of some sort. It was usually an insignificant issue blown out of proportion. Once as I was leaving the house to go teach a study, Cheryl shouted out to me to make sure that I (Mr. Spiritual) told the people how mean and rude I'd been to my wife. I don't remember if she used the word *hypocrite* but that was surely her implication. Just like all the other times, I headed into a teaching situation feeling the weight of conflict and accusation. It seemed unbearable and extremely discouraging.

This happened so consistently that I could predict when a blowup was coming. It always came a few hours before the Bible study. It finally dawned on me that this was more than a coincidence. It was also more than Brian and Cheryl having a spat—this was spiritual warfare!

Most Christians go years in their walk with the Lord unaware of this dimension of their spiritual lives. And because they're unaware of the spiritual battle they're in, they experience defeat over and over again. I remember as a young Christian suddenly having a change from joy, peace, and excitement to gloominess, confusion, and frustration. *What had happened?* I wondered. Why this heaviness all of the sudden? It was then that a friend clued me in to the fact that we are in a battle and it's not against flesh and blood, but against the devil and the forces of darkness. It took me a little longer to make that connection in relation to our marriage, but once I saw things for what they were I gained a whole new perspective on some of the struggles we were experiencing.

The Devil's Devices

By far, most of the problems I deal with in counseling are marital problems of one sort or another. Satan attacks marriages from all different angles. Sometimes the attack is subtle, other times it is blatant. Sometimes he just needles us with little irritating things until we explode at one another, other times he detonates a nuclear device that's intended to take us out instantly. We cannot afford to be "ignorant of his devices."

What are those devices? What tactics does the devil use in his war upon our marriages? Well, to begin with, anger, unforgiveness, and bitterness are right at the top of his list of things he will employ against us. These sins give the devil a foothold in the life of any person who harbors them, and that is certainly the case within the marital relationship as well. Because of that, the enemy is going to try to trap us in one or all of these sinful, destructive attitudes toward our spouses.

So many times I've seen these things playing a major role in failing marriages. Satan delights when we seethe in anger toward one another as husband and wife; he delights in our refusal to forgive one another from our hearts; and he senses victory when our petty bitterness is revealed. When he has a grip in our lives, he is at a greater advantage in his attempts to bring our marriages down.

We all get angry at times, but we must beware of holding on to that anger. Paul the apostle said, "Be angry and do not sin, do not let the sun go down on your wrath, nor give place to the devil." Satan will feed us all kinds of reasons why our anger is justified and why we shouldn't let it go. And often we embrace these reasons gladly. But know this: It's a trap! Watch it. Don't go there. Give the matter over to the Lord and ask Him for strength to deal with the situation.

I can think of many times I've been tempted to hold on to my anger toward Cheryl, or to withhold forgiveness from her over some disagreement or dispute we've had. At those times my mind is flooded with good and logical reasons why I should retain my anger: "She needs to learn a lesson here." "If I let her off the hook that easily she'll think that she can just do this anytime." "I'm not going to say I'm sorry—she's the one at fault here."

Does any of that sound familiar? That is the kind of reasoning the enemy loves and will take advantage of if we let him. When we provide a place for those kinds of thoughts in our mind, we are "giving place to the devil." We are setting ourselves up for a fall. When we feed and nurture those thoughts, we allow those resentments to become darker and darker. The next thing you know, a husband can imagine crossing from an emotional manifestation of his anger to a physical one. Or he fantasizes about finding another woman to replace his "difficult" wife. We open ourselves up to great loss each time we hold on to our anger and unforgiveness. Women will discover the same temptations and issues as they give a place for Satan's influence to settle into their thoughts.

While counseling Christian couples, I've watched as they've hurled accusation after accusation at one another. As the argument spirals downward, they dredge up failures, mistakes, or broken promises from 10, 20, or 30 years ago. People who once loved each other and at one time really enjoyed being together have become distant strangers who barely tolerate being in the same room. Such is the divisiveness of Satan's chains of bitterness and hatred.

My counsel for these couples is to stop accusing each other and to seek the help of the Holy Spirit (the only one who can help at that point) for the strength to forgive one another. Sadly, there have been too many times when that counsel has fallen on deaf ears. The next step is often the filing of divorce papers. How sad.

It doesn't have to be this way. Satan should never have the ultimate victory over any Christian marriage, and he won't if we recognize his tactics and fight him with the spiritual weapons God has given us. "If indeed I have forgiven anything, I have forgiven that one…in the presence of Christ, lest Satan should take advantage of us; for we are not ignorant of his devices" (2 Corinthians 2:10-11). Don't stew in your anger; don't hold on to unforgiveness; don't allow bitterness to take hold of you. Rather,

> as the elect of God, holy and beloved, put on tender mercies, kindness, humility, meekness, longsuffering; bearing with one another, and forgiving one another, if anyone has a complaint against another; even as Christ forgave you, so you also must do (Colossians 3:12-13).

A WORD TO THE MEN:

The Battle of Sexual Temptation

B There is one area of attack I want to highlight: temptation into sexual sin and adultery. Infidelity is many times the cause of a marital breakup. And in most cases, the man is the one who has succumbed to temptation and sinned. Let me remind you of the fact that the enemy, Satan, can manipulate our mind-sets, situations, and temptations to create the "perfect storm" in his attempts to wipe out our marriages.

First, he creates in us a discontent with our wives, our marriages, our careers, our lives in general. He prepares our hearts with further lust and discontentment as we catch sight of inappropriate images or choose to watch movies with nudity and sex. Our lust can grow and demand more from us as we feel compelled to turn to the Internet and its immediate access to pornography and communication with other women.

Then, at just the right moment, he sends his agent—that sweet, understanding, adoring, and good-looking woman—into your workplace, or next to you on the stationary bike at the gym, beside you at church (you're serving together on the worship team), or sometimes right into your home (you offered a listening ear to a woman and now she's flattering you and you're falling for it)!

I'm not making this stuff up. These things really happen. I could share many real-life horror stories straight from the front lines of pastoral ministry—men being led as "sheep to the slaughter" by immoral women who are nothing less than satanic agents of destruction. As I said, sometimes the enemy sets off a nuclear device hoping to take us out instantly. Adultery is like a nuclear explosion in a marriage. It leaves behind an emotional and spiritual wasteland for those who are affected by it.

Men, here is what you need to do with great diligence:

131

1. *Guard your heart;* out of it flows the makings of your life. Be careful that your emotions are never allowed to control your actions. (I don't feel like I love my wife anymore. I have feelings for this other woman.)

2. *Guard your mind.* Satan's primary attack is against our minds, and this is where he'll seek to get an advantage over us. He'll put into our minds evil thoughts and imaginations, hoping we will dwell on them, embrace them, and ultimately act on them.

3. *Guard your eyes.* Do not look lustfully or longingly at a woman who is not your wife. Stop the double take! Make a covenant, as Job did, with your eyes:

> Why...should I gaze upon a young woman? For what is the allotment of God from above, and the inheritance of the Almighty from on high? Is it not destruction for the wicked, and disaster for the workers of iniquity? Does He not see my ways, and count all my steps? (Job 31:1-4).

We are in a war. The stakes are high. Don't be ignorant of Satan's attack against your marriage. Resist him, standing steadfast in the faith. We'll address the topic of sex in more depth in another chapter, but I wanted to incorporate the vital issue of sexual sin in this chapter specifically. It is important to understand that as you make room for lust and longing in your heart, you are opening doors for more spiritual destruction and temptation to unfold.

Enlighten Your Marriage

C   There are times when the attack that we feel is a supernatural one. But how do we recognize when it is Satan or a mere squabble with our spouse? This is where enlightenment is essential.

Often false beliefs will cast a shadow over our thoughts. They might come as strong suggestions like, "You're really not being fulfilled in this relationship." "Your spouse is just not there for you."

Years ago, a friend of mine was ready to leave her husband. When I asked her what the issue was she said, "He's just not there for me." I asked her to clarify what she meant but she couldn't. I tried to help her by asking specifics. In every area I mentioned, her husband more than met her expectations. In the end, she realized she had no basis for her conclusion.

How many men and women start their path of sin with the slow burn of discontentment? From there, we are more than happy to fuel the flame as we embrace the devil's whispers of "something better" or his equally seductive lies about not being "good enough" for a healthy, whole, godly life. So whether our ego is inflated or our self-worth is trampled upon, we are primed for Satan's power to influence us.

A WORD TO THE WOMEN:
History of Women and Warfare

Personally, I think the enemy works on women's vulnerabilities especially. Remember the Garden of Eden? We are not told whether Satan had any conversations with Adam. Why? Because if he did have a conversation with Adam, it was unsuccessful. Paul states, "Adam was not deceived, but the woman being deceived, fell into transgression." That is not to say that men are exempt from spiritual warfare—it is only to say that the ways Satan attempts to manipulate women are different than the means he uses on men.

In Genesis 2 the first marriage is presented to us. It seems like a great union. After all, Eve was tailor-made for Adam! God looks at this union and blesses it, saying, "Be fruitful and multiply; fill the earth and subdue it." Then He "saw everything that He had made, and indeed it was very good" (Genesis 1:28,31). That was the original state of the first and original relationship between man and wife.

How long Adam and Eve continued in this state, we are not told. What we are told is that Satan, disguised as a harmless serpent, started conversing with Eve. He began by questioning her about God's directives. "Has God indeed said, 'You shall not eat of every tree of the garden'?"

Satan initiated the conversation by pointing out and questioning the limitations in Eve's life. He also questioned the validity of God's word. Eve had heard the directive from Adam. She repeated it as she knew it: "We may eat of the fruit of the trees of the garden; but of the fruit of the tree which is in the midst of the garden, God has said, 'You shall not eat it, nor shall you touch it, lest you die.'"

She had already corrupted what the Lord had told Adam. God's exact words were, "Of every tree of the garden you may freely eat; but of the tree of the knowledge of good and evil you shall not eat, for in the day that you eat of it you shall surely die." Do you see the difference? Eve had added just a bit to God's word by saying, "nor shall you touch it." She had also lessened the degree of danger by saying, "lest you die" rather than "you shall surely die." Having moved away from God's direct word, she was even more susceptible to the suggestions of the devil.

Next the devil suggested that God's word had no power. God had said that on the day that they ate of the fruit they would "surely die." Satan directly contradicted God's word by saying, "You will not surely die."

As Eve entertained the enemy's lies without a secure grasp on God's word, she began to eye the forbidden fruit with longing. Before her was the idea that she could do what was forbidden and suffer no negative consequence.

Finally, the devil told Eve that the forbidden fruit held promise for her. He implied that by eating it, her life would be enhanced and she would be like God, knowing good from evil. He further implied that God's only real objection to her eating the fruit would be that she would become godlike. If that isn't a temptation for the ego, what is?

You might say Eve bit on the lie! It was she, not Adam, who believed the lie first and partook of what was forbidden.

The devil still tries to converse with women by presenting them with false promises. Take for instance the temptations my good friend Donna faced. Donna was struggling in her marriage. Her husband was inattentive to her needs. He was still bemoaning the breakup of his first marriage and wasn't ready to put the same emotional investment into his present one. Donna was unhappy but committed to the relationship in obedience to God's Word.

One day, as she sat alone drinking a latte at a coffee shop, a handsome man approached her. He looked at her sympathetically and asked if she was happy. Donna gave him a half smile and nodded her head unconvincingly.

The man began to compliment her. He said that he sensed in her some unhappiness. He told her that God loved her deeply and had great plans for her life. Her heart began to warm to his words.

He then asked if he could take a seat at her table. Donna gestured with her hand toward an open seat. The man took the seat and set his cup down. He looked into her eyes and said, "You don't have to stay in this marriage. There are better options out there for you. You need someone who will really love you and take care of you."

His words were smooth and pleasant, but Donna felt something distressing in her heart. "Lord, give me discernment," her heart prayed.

"I am committed to the Lord Jesus," she announced to the man. He grimaced. "I am also committed to the marriage God gave me," she continued.

At this the man drew back. He gave her a look of utter disdain. His whole demeanor transformed itself before her.

"Fine!" he snarled. "You will never be happy!" He rose from the table and walked out the door, leaving Donna in a state of bewilderment.

What just happened? she muttered to herself. The answer came to her immediately. She had been talking to the devil. Not the prince of darkness himself, but it had been his words in the man's mouth. It was the devil's suggestions she had been hearing. She shook with fright at how close she had come to giving her life over to the devil's offerings.

It was only a month later that a huge breakthrough erupted in her marriage. She and her husband had a long talk that ended with both of them on their knees rededicating their individual lives and their marriage to God. After that prayer of consecration, everything changed. Today, Donna and her husband serve happily together in ministry and in marriage.

When you are at your most vulnerable physically, mentally, or spiritually, the devil is more easily able to capture your attention and point out your longings, your broken dreams, and all that is wrong in your life. Don't let go of God's hope and grace in exchange for the delusions and destructive whispers of the devil.

Recognizing the Devil and His Lies

C Unfortunately, the devil doesn't wear an obvious costume. He doesn't introduce himself by listing his intentions to destroy you, your marriage, and your faith. So how do we know when we are encountering darkness?

Paul the apostle says that Satan transforms himself as an angel of light (2 Corinthians 11:14). So if he is disguised, how are we supposed to know when we are engaging with him? We know by the content of what is being suggested. In John 8:44, Jesus said that the devil is a liar and always has been. Lying is what the devil does "because there is no truth in him. When he speaks a lie, he speaks from his own resources, for he is a liar and the father of it."

The Devil's Lie Number One

The first lie the devil will put forth is that God's Word cannot be trusted. He will subtly ask concerning your situation, "Did God really say…?" Of course, in the context of what we are talking about, it will have something to do with your marriage. He will question the validity of God's Word about marriage. Concealed in that suggestion will also be the validity of the limitations given in God's Word, and therefore the limitations in your marriage.

For instance, he might question your understanding of fidelity in marriage. He might ask, "Do you have to be with just this one person for the rest of your life?" Or he might ask, "What did God really say about marriage? Does He really expect you to be committed to your marriage? Does He really expect you to submit?" The enemy will ask these and other questions that cast aspersions on what God has said in the Bible about marriage.

The best preparation for these attacks is to know and understand what God has said about marriage in His Word. Read firsthand what He has said. I suggest you read and meditate on the following verses:

- Genesis 2:18-24
- Proverbs 18:1
- Malachi 2:14-16
- Matthew 5:31-32
- Matthew 19:3-9
- Ephesians 5:22-33
- 1 Peter 2:20–3:8
- Hebrews 13:4

This is not an all-inclusive list of scriptures that deal with what God says about marriage, but it will give you a clear picture of His heart and purpose for your union.

My friend Donna was able to recognize the devil's lies in the words of the man at the coffee shop because she knows the Word of God. This was her first line of resistance. As she stood in God's Word, the devil left. As you stand in the Word of God, you will recognize the subtle suggestions of the enemy and be able to resist.

Satan's Second Lie

The next suggestion of Satan is twofold. Not only does he suggest that we can sin and not suffer consequences, but he impresses upon us a false belief that God's Word is not trustworthy. Remember that God said, "In the day that you eat of it you will surely die." Satan told Eve, "You will not surely die." What a lie! From the moment she ate the forbidden fruit, death began working in her and then in Adam when he ate. The consequences of that death were and are manifold!

The pair suddenly felt vulnerable. They were scared. They hid from the presence of God. They were cast out of the garden. They lived by their toil. Their son murdered his brother. Since Adam and Eve, every person can be sure of the inevitability of death.

So Satan whispers to our heart that we can play with sin, flirtations, and lascivious thoughts, and our marriage will not suffer for it. Hah! It's a downright lie.

There are ramifications and far-reaching results of disobeying God's commands. He doesn't give us advice on marriage—He gives us commands that, if followed, will give us blessed marriages. However, if we violate those commands, we may be assured that death will work in every area of our lives, including marriage.

God's ways work. They might take a bit longer—no doubt that is why His Word also tells us to "wait on the Lord." When I decided to follow His Word in my marriage, I didn't see immediate results. In fact, at times it really did seem as though His ways did not work. His Word didn't conform Brian into the image of the husband I wanted. No… but it conformed him into the image of the husband *God* wanted for me and the husband I needed.

The devil will also suggest that prayer doesn't work. He will tell you that submission will be disastrous. He will tell you that you must be contentious or nothing will go right (Proverbs 21:9). Each lie Satan whispers to your mind and heart will require you to walk in opposition to God's Word and ways.

As I mentioned, the way to recognize these suggestions is to know what God's instructions concerning marriage are. This will require going back and reviewing what God says about marriage in His Word.

Next, you will have to resist these suggestions by choosing to do things God's way. This act will require faith, which means you will have to believe God's Word not only above what Satan is saying, but also even above the circumstances. As you learn to resist the devil's lies and dedicate yourself to following God's directives, you will see Him begin to honor obedience to His Word by working in your marriage.

The Devil's Third Deception

Satan told Eve that in the day she ate of the forbidden fruit she would be godlike. In other words he was suggesting that she would find fulfillment in sin. His intimation was that God didn't care about her fulfillment. Rather, He cared only about retaining His superiority over her.

This lie needs closer examination. This is one of the devil's greatest ploys: suggesting to women that God is not interested in their personal fulfillment. Nothing could be further from the truth. Jesus said in John 10:10 that He came to bring us life and that more abundantly. He also said that the thief comes only to rob and to steal.

God's ways are the ways of fulfillment. Remember the woman at the well in John 4. She had tried to do marriage and relationships and had been left unfulfilled. She had drunk the water of this world and been left thirsty. Jesus promised her that if she asked Him for the water He gave, she would never be thirsty again.

Often I have heard women almost apologize for their husbands, saying, "I could have done better than him." I am never impressed with that notion. I always counter that I know that Brian is God's gift to me—and you can't do better than God's gift! I believe that whenever either partner thinks they could have done better than the spouse they have, someone has been conversing with the devil.

Fulfillment doesn't come in disobeying the commands of God, which is what the enemy implies. Fulfillment is not found in an extramarital affair or in a new mate. Fulfillment is in doing marriage God's way.

I want to reiterate that Satan's suggestions come disguised. They often take the form of foreign feelings, which is to say, emotions we have not felt before. They also come as thoughts we have not considered before. That is why it is so important to measure every thought that comes into our mind before dwelling on it or letting it develop any further. The apostle John states in his epistle, "Beloved, do not believe every spirit, but test the spirits, whether they are of God; because many false prophets have gone out into the world" (1 John 4:1). In the same manner we must test our thoughts against the Word of God before we entertain them.

That is our first line of defense—testing such thoughts with the Word of God. Next we take those same thoughts to the Lord in prayer and thus into submission to Him and His Word (2 Corinthians 10:5). Finally, we make a conscious choice not to entertain them.

I have found the best way to avoid thinking about something is to choose to pray about something else. When a particularly troubling thought comes to my mind, I immediately pray for a specific situation I have already resolved to pray for. When a thought comes to me that has the potential to harm my marriage, I pray for a friend who has cancer. If I can't get over being mad at something Brian says, I pray for a wonderful church I'm familiar with in York, England.

Causing Trouble

Brian mentioned early in this chapter that there have been times when, right before he speaks, a quarrel has broken out between us. That's absolutely true. Suddenly, a thought (watch those things!) will come to me about Brian, our marriage, or a certain issue between us, and I feel an urgency to get it resolved right then and there. Poor Brian. He is trying to concentrate on what he is to say to God's people.

As I learned to recognize the sources of my thoughts, I began to realize which were authentic and which were inspired by the devil. I learned not to act on them until I had checked them with the Word and prayed. I wish I could say I never act on a wrong thought anymore, but that would make me divine, and I can guarantee you I am not divine!

I vividly recall numerous occasions when my excited preparations for a getaway with Brian were marred by some petty argument that seemed monumental at the time. One time, it was a phone call we were expecting. It came about 5:00 in the morning. I heard Brian mumbling into the phone something about meeting them at the hospital. Immediately I jumped out of bed. "Is the baby on the way?" I practically screamed with joy.

Sleepily Brian turned over in bed and in garbled words told me they would call us when the baby was born.

"What! No way! That's my baby having a baby. I am going to the hospital with or without you!"

Now the whole household was awake. Groggily our two youngest made their way into our room, asking if their older sister was in labor. When I told them she was, they jumped excitedly up and down, irritating the sleeping giant.

Sitting up in bed, Brian asked me what I thought I could do at the hospital while Kristyn was in labor. "A girl needs her mother at times like this," I replied. "I can storm the hallways and pray."

Reluctantly, Brian drove me to the hospital at 6:00 a.m. We were both silent. What should have been a ride of joy was awkwardly silent. We were both seething at each other and convinced that we held the right position.

When we got to the hospital we found Kristyn and Michael walking the halls while the room was being prepared. Suddenly she turned to me and said, "I can't do this anymore."

I knew then that she had to get to her room right away. It was time. During this flurry of activity, Brian was sitting in the waiting room, probably wishing he was at home in bed. But as soon as we needed him, he was ready and willing. I'm easily intimidated by nurses and doctors, but my husband isn't. So I sent him in to our daughter's room to help.

Brian returned a few minutes later. His face was ashen. "She needs her mother."

I quickly made my way to the delivery room, Brian following. I did what moms do. I sprang into action to help my daughter. I found a washcloth and began to dab the sweat from Kristyn's forehead. I counted down her contractions and got her to focus. I helped Michael work with her. Then I informed the nurse that my daughter, who is immune to pain, was in transition.

The nurse informed the doctor, who was incredulous. However, at my insistence, he checked Kristyn and found that the baby was crowning. I stepped out in the hallway with Brian. He looked sheepish and whispered an apology.

I realized that we had almost allowed dark thoughts to extinguish the joy of one of the greatest, brightest moments of our lives. Brian and I held hands and prayed. In a few moments we heard the healthy cry of a newborn baby resounding from Kristyn's room. Then we joined in with tears of joy!

Prepared to Protect Your Joy

It seems that the devil is always there to try to steal the joy from what God intends to be the greatest moments of our lives. In the Bible, Solomon talked about the little foxes that steal the grapes. Often it is not the big things that rob our joy, but the trivial ones. It might be a word, a look, or an attitude that suddenly transforms a special moment, memory, or opportunity into regret and loss.

If our spouse is suffering from agitation and destructive practices, we need to recognize it as spiritual warfare and pray for them. That is the only effective way to deal with it. If we are the one suffering from those eruptions and deceptions, we need to develop sensitivity to what it feels like to be out of line with godly emotions and responses. This will allow us to recognize and change our behavior with and in God's strength and power.

Warfare comes in all different size packages. It is important to recognize it in whatever size it comes and resist it by giving it over to the Lord in prayer and refusing to give in to it.

The devil hates your marriage and wants to destroy it. God loves your marriage and wants to bless it. It's that simple.

KNOWING IS GROWING

1. Which of Satan's lies have you bought into? Have you believed that you deserve better than you have…or that you are not worthy of what you have? Talk about this with your spouse. Which side of Satan's coin of dissatisfaction do you tend to believe? Knowing this about yourself and your spouse will help you guard your heart against deception.

2. As we shared about our fights and conflicts that would come up right before Brian was about to teach or lead a Bible study, did this raise any red flags about your own circumstances? Do you tend to fight or erupt in rage when one of you is about to do something for the Lord? Think about this and pray over each other so you have an awareness and deliberately guard your hearts and minds during these trigger times. How can you defuse the devil's work during these situations? Come up with a game plan to put into action this week.

3. Sometimes discontentment in a marriage is born of Satan's lies. Sometimes it is born of our own weaknesses or times of neglect. Take time to evaluate where your marriage is weakest and most prone to breeding a sense of dissatisfaction. How can you nurture this area specifically with God's Word, prayer, and focused effort? Your areas of discontentment may not be the same trouble areas for your spouse. That is why this conversation is important to have. You might not realize that your spouse never feels heard. You might be clueless that when

you joke with your spouse, their feelings are hurt. Take time to understand each other so you give Satan less and less to work with!

Growing-Together Grace

God, You are our source of life and light. Please cast Your light on the deceptions of the devil we have allowed into our marriage. Show us, for every point of discontent or failure, how we can become victorious in Your might and mercy. Enlighten us, Lord. Illuminate those times when we argue and fight and are likely to destroy something good and godly You are preparing.

When are we undermining Your work? Open our eyes to our weakest areas so we can pray with specificity against Satan's plots and plans. Guard our hearts, minds, eyes, spirits, and lives, Lord. And bless this marriage. May we serve You and one another all of our days.

Essential EIGHT:
Energize

Let the husband render to his wife the affection due her, and likewise also the wife to her husband. The wife does not have authority over her own body, but the husband does. And likewise, the husband does not have authority over his own body, but the wife does.

1 CORINTHIANS 7:3-4

Energize

Sex, sex, sex! The world has gone mad over sex! Since the so-called Sexual Revolution of the 1960s and 1970s, sex has taken a prominent place in American culture's priorities and consciousness. In previous generations, discussion of sexual issues was limited pretty much to the bedroom, but today, talk of sex is everywhere: the Internet, the television, the cinema, the theater, the radio, the newsstand, the classroom, the playground, the courtroom and, more frequently these days, even the pulpit.

As you well know, it isn't just talk these days. Sexually provocative images bombard us from every quarter. Don't you marvel at how far advertisers will go in their attempts to appeal to consumers? To see a scantily clad woman stroking a rebuilt transmission is about as far over the top as you can get! Such ads go after women as well. How many times have we seen a shirtless, sweating (glistening) guy with six-pack abs as the focal point in an ad for women's soft drinks or diet aids? The message is, "This is who will be attracted to you as soon as you buy our product."

We are a sex-obsessed culture, yet believe it or not, we are still somewhat restrained in comparison to other places. In various parts of Europe, it is not at all uncommon to see hard-core pornographic images on billboards throughout the cities. And during the warmer months, beaches are packed with nude sunbathers.

Being bombarded with sexually charged images and opportunities can affect for ill the way we think about sex and how we relate to one another as husband and wife. This is why it's important that we understand God's purpose in creating us with sexual desires and His intentions for our sexual enjoyment within the marital relationship.

You probably noticed that we said, "God's purpose in creating us with sexual desires." The desire for sexual pleasure, in and of itself, is not wrong or dirty or sinful—it is a part of the way He made us. Sex becomes wrong or sinful only when it is taken outside of its God-ordained boundaries. Sex is something He is very strict about. Apparently our sexuality is such an important part of our humanity that He has not left it up to us to set the rules regarding our sexual activity. That is something He's reserved for Himself.

This is one of the most offensive aspects of the Bible's teaching to the modern mind. "How dare anyone suggest that there is a God who is going to tell me what I can and can't do with my body!" cries the modernist. They can protest all they want, but God's Word is fixed and it can't be altered. And do you know what? We should delight in this truth because sex is God's gift to His creatures. It is His gift to those sharing in the marriage covenant.

There are many joys and benefits to sex that God has envisioned and purposed for our marriages. We'll explore how and why sexual and emotional intimacy is essential for any marriage where husband and wife are growing together spiritually.

How Guilt Entered the Bedroom

In the early stages of the history of the church, ascetic beliefs arose, declaring that all experiences of pleasure were essentially evil because of their connection with the material world. Sadly, this ideology crept into the godly marriage bed, and the sexual relationship between a husband and wife was declared to be only for the purpose of reproduction. Sex for the purpose of enjoyment was considered wrong and sinful.

This false teaching is in total contradiction to the teaching of Scripture, and yet it continues to rob more people of the blessing God intended for the sexual relationship than almost anything else. These ideas have so permeated our Christian culture that even the Sexual Revolution's influence did not erase the hang-ups and guilt many men and women hold on to about having sex with their spouses simply for the pleasure and fun of it. This is a great loss to the marital relationship. And this loss has caused sex to become a divide in marriages rather than the uniting intimacy God intended.

You can see how Satan has been busy all these centuries trying to create confusion over this issue and then driving people to one extreme or the other. Some say, "To heck with the rules—I'll do whatever I want!" Others live in bondage and fear of judgment, restricting themselves and their spouses in ungodly ways and missing out on the wonderful gift of intimacy God has given. As is always the case, His Word brings the perfect balance. Sex is His gift to a married couple to freely enjoy as often as their hearts desire.

Consider how the Garden of Eden was filled with a variety of abundant, lush trees for Adam and Eve to enjoy without limit. They were there for their nourishment and pleasure. There was only one restriction—the tree in the middle of the garden was off limits. They could not eat from it. They had all they needed, and so much more, from the countless trees that were given to them freely. God provided and provided in great abundance for their delight. But we all know how the story goes...all that God had given was perceived as not enough. Adam and Eve couldn't resist the *one* tree.

We can learn a lot from Adam and Eve about our sexual relations with our spouse! We can have all the fruit of sexual pleasure within our marriage, but we can't partake outside the boundaries and best interests of the marital relationship. Just as the eating of the forbidden tree in Eden brought death, so taking sex outside God's designated boundaries results in death in some form. We destroy trust, faith, unity, and the purity of the pleasure intended only for husband and wife.

Boundaries for Blessing

Since sex is God's good gift to be enjoyed as often as we like within the boundary of the marital relationship, is there anything that is prohibited sexually between a husband and wife? Let me answer that as discreetly as possible. But first let me say, I don't believe that it's good or necessary or wise to go into graphic details when we talk about sex. There are some teachers today who, in their attempt to be culturally relevant and apparently prove that Christians are not the puritanical prudes we've been accused of being, go way over the top in writing and speaking on the subject of sex. As my younger daughter would say, "TMI"—too much information! I'm of the firm belief that people can figure out on their own how to enjoy each other sexually. After all, we (humans) have been doing this from the beginning.

If we turn to God's Word, we do find guidance and inspiration. I consider the Song of Solomon to be somewhat of a manual on romantic love between a husband and wife. And the statement in Hebrews 13:4 that says the bed is undefiled within the context of marriage seems to allow for sexual experimentation between husband and wife. In other words, be free to enjoy each other totally. But your experimentation should be mutually consensual.

A WORD TO THE MEN:

Becoming a Godly Lover

B While women like intimacy to be nurtured throughout the day with small signs of affection and close connections in conversation and partnership, we men don't depend so much on the accumulation of affection. We just see our wives looking good, and we are ready to go! We sometimes seem little different than beasts! "I see, I like, I want, and that's that!" However, actually stating this or acting like this is the surest way I know of to turn off my wife to the thought of being intimate with me.

For that reason, sexual boundaries or courtesies are indispensable. You may know these, but let's explore why they are important.

1. *Never demand or try to force your wife to do something sexually she's uncomfortable with.* Don't ask her to do anything that makes her feel guilty, dirty, or like she's just an object rather than a person.

2. *Don't allow anything unnatural into the intimate area of your lives.* I know of situations where men have wanted to bring pornography into the bedroom to help "liven things up." If I tried something like that my wife would kick me where it hurts and lock me out of the bedroom permanently. And she would be completely justified in doing it! Don't bring sinful exploitations into your life. Don't bring them into your personal thought life (or beyond), and do not bring them into your marriage.

3. *Show your wife considerate, loving actions along with tender expressions of your love for her.* I have learned that this is the best way to assure that my wife will desire to be with me intimately. It starts early in the morning by getting her favorite kind of coffee. I continue to show her my love throughout the day by doing little things here and there. As we move toward the evening, we are connected and there is a foundation of loving intimacy. You'll discover that you will enjoy this fostering of intimacy as well.

4. *If you want romance be romantic, don't be beastly.* Make sure that before you approach your wife, you are groomed…showered, shaved, teeth brushed, and so on. Now, there will be times when none of that matters and you'll both just be hungry for one another, even after a weekend of camping or a long day of working in the yard. But as a general rule, don't be a

beast, be a prince—and you'll find that your wife will be more than willing to share herself with you freely and abundantly.

5. *Keep your sex life private.* I know guys who, for whatever reason, like to describe their sexual exploits in detail. I don't know that there could be anything more humiliating to a wife than to find out that her husband is talking publicly about their private lives. Respect your wife in this area. Guard her privacy. This will increase her security in your love and give her more freedom to enjoy that part of your lives. Also know that when guys do a lot of bragging or talking about this area, most other men find it uncomfortable, inappropriate, and insensitive.

When the Lord said, "The two shall become one," He was referring to a union far deeper than simply the physical one. As much as God has given the sexual relationship to us for our physical enjoyment, it is also intended to be an emotional and spiritual connection. In this place and time of intimacy, your emotional needs are met in ways that I don't even fully understand. I do know that this is one area that I share with no one but Cheryl; that alone makes it very special and precious.

A WORD TO THE WOMEN:

Protecting Your Heart

Women naturally feel vulnerable. One of the greatest needs of a woman is to feel secure and protected. The more secure, loved, and protected a woman is, the more freely she will be able to express her love in the confines of the bedroom.

Men often take their wife's sexual refusal personally, not realizing that in the majority of cases it has very little to do with them. It has to do with her insecurities. Consider those awful magazine covers. What do you think it feels like to be an aging woman with leftover pregnancy bulges confronted daily by women who are young, beautiful, flat in the right places, and voluptuous in the other places? It makes us feel insecure and even unsure about our potential to be attractive to our husbands. These insecurities are carried right into the bedroom.

One evening years ago, Brian and I stepped out to enjoy our wedding anniversary. Our date began in a hotel room, where Brian stepped into the shower. On the way to the hotel, we were both giddy with excitement about getting to spend some much needed romantic time together. We held hands, kissed, and said quite a few endearments to each other.

While Brian showered, I turned on the television and watched whatever was on at the time. After all, I didn't want any part of my outfit to become wrinkled while he cleaned up. The TV lit up with a particular talk show where the hostess was interviewing a model. The model was dressed mysteriously in a trench coat.

During the interview, the host tried to coax the beautiful model to take off her coat. "I can't," the model gushed in a breathy European accent. "The women watching would all hate me. They know their husbands would rather have me than them, and it makes them angry with me."

After the host prodded her one more time, the model removed her coat. She was wearing a bikini—barely. She had all the right curves in all the right places. I grimaced as I thought of my own post-baby frame.

As I watched this spectacle, I became incensed at the model, the hostess, and men in general. I heard Brian finish his shower, so I quickly turned off the show. But my thoughts remained fixed on the absurd interview.

Brian hummed blissfully in the background and I fumed over the display of inappropriateness. The more I thought about what I had seen, the more my thoughts became illogical. They spiraled away from anything godly or sensible: *If that model is what men really want, she is just what Brian really wants. What is he doing with me? He'd much rather have a beautiful, perfect model from Europe! Well, if he wants her, he can have her! I don't need a man. I don't need rejection.*

At that moment, Brian entered the room dressed, radiant, and smelling like citrus and spice. Smiling broadly he asked if I was ready to go to dinner.

"Sure," I answered icily.

Not catching the coldness in my voice, Brian inquired about where we should dine. "Does it even matter what I say? You're the man—it's all about fulfilling your desire of where you want to eat!" I said haughtily.

He looked at me quizzically. "Cheryl, I am not sure what just happened. I know that we were in love before I stepped into the shower. While I was showering, I was under the impression that we were happily married and going to have a wonderful night celebrating our marriage. I shaved, brushed my teeth, put on cologne, dressed, and came out here to see my beautiful wife—"

"Beautiful?" I snarled.

My husband looked at me and then at the television. Walking purposefully toward it, he put his hand on the screen. "It's warm. What were you watching?"

"I was watching a talk show with the woman you really want to have."

"What are you talking about?" he countered.

I answered his question with a lively account of what I had just witnessed along with a confession of all of my drastic and dramatic assumptions.

"Cheryl, I don't even know that model," Brian began, "but I can assure you I don't want her. I want you. You are the one that God gave to me as my wife, my soul mate, my best friend, the mother of my children. I think that woman and that show became a chance for the devil to ruin our evening."

And just like that, his words broke the spell. I couldn't believe how gullible I had been. I had allowed my insecurities to short-circuit the start of our romantic night. All it took was the image of a beautiful woman in a bikini, and the devil had me interpreting this as a threat to my value, to my worth, and to Brian's faithfulness.

What do you allow to take hold of your thoughts and sense of value? When do your thoughts spiral downward? These insecurities, as I mentioned before, carry into the bedroom and jeopardize a fulfilling and blessed relationship between you and your husband.

Once I picked up a magazine and began to read an article entitled "What a Wife Could Learn from a Mistress." It was written by a woman who had been engaged in a 20-year affair with a married man. She had quite a few opinions to offer married women about how to keep their husbands happy. I had only gotten to the third paragraph when I felt the gentle prodding of the Holy Spirit reminding me, "Blessed is the man who walks not in the counsel of the ungodly" (Psalm 1:1). This woman had nothing to say to me that I needed or wanted to hear. The only advice and guidance that nurtures marriage is from God.

The "voice" of the world needs to be shut out of the bedroom. By protecting this intimate place from the outside world, you will learn to trust only God's leading. And as you grow together, you will both feel loved and accepted.

There is a need to keep the bedroom strictly private! Don't let any images or stories enter into this very intimate time between you and your husband. The bedroom becomes blessed when no outside images are allowed in. When no comparisons are made. But this isn't easy for men or women. We can grow together as couples when we nurture a sense of love, commitment, faithfulness, affection, and devotion.

Intimacy Issues

The young wife sat across from me, her embarrassment obvious in her downcast eyes, her red cheeks. She spoke softly and deliberately with long pauses between words. Her hands seemed to wrestle with one another as she tried to keep them still in her lap. She shifted uncomfortably from side to side.

"Well…it's like this…" she said staring down at her feet, avoiding eye contact. "My…uh…husband…talked to your husband…Brian. Brian told him that I…uh…needed to come talk to you."

From her posture alone I could guess why my counsel had been invoked. "Does your husband want you to talk to me because the areas of intimacy in your marriage are not going well?"

Her head shot up and she looked me in the eyes. "Yes," she almost sobbed.

Immediately I assured her, "It happens to just about every Christian couple I know. Let me explain."

I began to paint a scenario repeated in many Christian households. In the beginning, the young wife is captivated by her husband. She can't get enough of his embrace. But after a few years of growing together as a couple, the business of marriage sets in. Perhaps the couple purchases a house, gets too occupied with their jobs or the calling on their life—and then they have children. Suddenly there are bills to be paid, a house to clean and manage, and young lives to be tended. Romance is replaced with duty.

At the same time, the wife begins to redefine herself by the demands on her life rather than by the man she married. She becomes the CEO of her household, the administrator of family affairs, the on-call nurse, the housekeeper, the bookkeeper, the counselor, and the virtuous mother. Even as she is redefining herself, the image of her handsome hero is also changing. He no longer smells like citrus and exotic spices (the cologne was no doubt relegated to the unnecessary expense list), his breath is rarely fresh and minty, his Hercules-like physique has softened in the middle, and he no longer romances his wife but rather makes bedroom demands of her, seemingly after the most hectic of days. This combination of life demands and the changing identities of husband and wife wreaks havoc on the sexual relationship.

To the woman who is engrossed in the business of marriage, intimacy with her husband becomes another household chore, like doing the dishes and making dinner. The husband interprets this as rejection and becomes either withdrawn or more demanding. The more the husband demands or requests intimacy, the less inclined the wife is toward it. The romantic aspect of their relationship is being lost in a sea of miscommunications, busy lifestyles, and changing identities.

As I explained this common dilemma for married couples, the young wife looked at me with astonishment. "You've just told my story," she said. "But what can I do?"

"The answer is simple," I comforted her. "In fact it is so simple that it is often neglected. The answer is to pray."

"Pray?"

"Yes. Pray for God to bless the intimate aspects of your marriage. Pray for God to give you desire for your husband. He wants your marriage to have a fulfilling sexual relationship. It is He who created marriage and created this intimate aspect of it for the mutual fulfillment of both the husband and the wife."

Bringing Sanctity Back to the Bedroom

C So how do we bring the sanctity back to the bedroom? As mentioned before, it begins with prayer. Next the bedroom must be cleared of all other voices and images so both partners feel safe. Finally, there needs to be preparation. I love the image in Song of Solomon of the Shulamite woman perfuming her bed for her husband's arrival.

Women love to be prepared. Plan for times together. This doesn't mean that there can't be spontaneity. There should be both. However, sometimes it is good to set the scene, like the Shulamite woman does. Mention to your husband that you want to spend some private time with him, or ask him to let you know when he wants time with you. And men, pay attention to the signals, the subtle comments, and the straightforward ideas your wife is sharing.

Plan on reviving your affection for one another or strengthening it. Start by listening to one another. Women, share with your husband the things that make you know he loves you. Your husband wants to bless you and he needs your advice and help on how to inspire and attract you. So be open with him and let these bits of personal information become your secrets together.

Husbands, share with your wife what you love about holding her hand or how you like it when you are sitting in the living room together just reading or talking. Let her know what you enjoy and delight in so you grow together through your daily intimacies as well as through your sexual relationship.

The Necessity of Intimacy

Years ago, Brian and I had gotten thoroughly engrossed in the business of marriage and ministry, as I described to the young woman above. We also had neglected this very important aspect of our marriage. It was actually our anniversary, but both of us had been too occupied with tasks and busyness, and Brian was now spending the evening studying in his office. Earlier in the day, we had been short with each other and the tension had mounted. Alone in the bedroom upstairs, it dawned on me—we needed each other. But I wanted him to initiate it. I waited until I couldn't take it any longer. Then I marched down to his office and announced that I wanted to celebrate our anniversary.

Brian practically leapt from his chair and followed me upstairs. The rest is private, but I want to say that the tension was broken and marital harmony was restored. We also both learned a valuable lesson that day, and that lesson was that the sexual aspect of intimacy was not to be neglected.

One of the reasons that sexual intimacy is often neglected is because one or the other partner considers it simply a pleasure rather than an essential of marriage. But it is essential to both husband and wife. The wife needs intimacy to reconnect with her husband and to get on the same page. The husband also needs to connect to his wife. Intimacy helps a man feel loved, wanted, and secure in the relationship with his wife. A wise Christian woman I knew gave me this piece of advice when I got married: "A husband feels loved when he is fed and fulfilled in the bedroom." How right she was. And a woman feels loved when she is cherished, protected, and delighted in by the man she adores.

The Spiritual Nature of Intimacy

The fact that the sexual relationship in marriage was both created and ordained by God eludes many couples. Some of this is due to the exploitation of sex in our culture. We become numb to the beauty and sanctity of the marriage bed. The devil has hijacked God's blessing of intimacy between married partners and corrupted it to the point that at times its spiritual aspect is unrecognizable. It is God who ordained marriage. It is He who created the sexual union between a husband and wife. The Bible states in Hebrews 13:4 that "marriage is honorable among all, and the marriage bed undefiled."

The apostle Paul speaks of this very vital aspect of marriage:

> Let the husband render to his wife the affection due her, and likewise also the wife to her husband. The wife does

not have authority over her own body, but the husband does. And likewise, the husband does not have authority over his own body, but the wife does. Do not deprive one another except with consent for a time, that you may give yourselves to fasting and prayer; and come together again so that Satan does not tempt you because of your lack of self-control (1 Corinthians 7:3-5).

Isn't this interesting? The chosen apostle of God is talking about the necessity of sexual intimacy in marriage. He goes so far as to state that it wards off the temptations of the devil.

Prayer brings the blessing of God into this area of marriage. Prayer changes the hearts and attitudes of husband and wife toward each other. Prayer purifies the bedroom and sanctifies the relationship of husband and wife. Prayer makes intimacy in marriage a sacred, precious act of love and devotion rather than a duty or a means of self-gratification.

Sexual intimacy is an essential aspect of every great Christian marriage. God wants to bless this area of your life as much as any other aspect. Recognizing the spirituality of this time, as well as the sanctity and need, will bring fulfillment and glory to your marriage relationship.

KNOWING IS GROWING

1. Plan a relaxed evening that allows you both a chance to have a safe, close conversation about your sexual relationship. Don't put pressure on yourselves to discuss or resolve or explore all aspects of your intimacy, but do open the dialogue to include loving words and conversation about what makes you each feel the most comfortable before and during sex. Talk about what inspires affection and connection between the two of you. Let there be laughter and times of quiet as you sit together. Reminisce about your first kiss or the first time you held hands. The sweetness of those simple expressions of love is a great reminder of what a delightful gift physical closeness is in your marriage.

2. How can you keep the world out of your bedroom? Evaluate the actual space and free it of the world. Get the television, computer, and home library of DVDs out. Decide how to cultivate a place that is restful, private, and personal. Don't make it a place to talk on the phone, read or send text messages, or finish work projects. A sanctuary will bring rest to your times of rest and energy to your times of intimacy.

3. Talk about what might energize your love life. Are you overburdened? Overworked? Stressed? Discuss ways you can lighten your load and rev up your energy for times together. Make a list of three things you'd like to incorporate into your daily or weekly lives so you can delight in lovemaking more easily. Go for daily walks. Turn off the television an hour before bed and sit and read together or talk (but not about money or other problem areas). Commit to joining a gym or eating more healthily. The healthier you are physically, the healthier your mind-set will be when it is time to focus on your loved one.

GROWING-TOGETHER GRACE

God, please protect our marital bed from outside influences. Give us both a sense of the joy and pleasure You intended for our intimate relationship. Release us from guilt, past mistakes, false thinking, low self-esteem, and the world's tainted view of sex. Free us from all that distracts so we can embrace the rich rewards of a loving, caring, passionate physical connection that helps us grow together as man and wife.

Lord, may we always be kind and attentive to one another. May we serve each other with Your unconditional love. Every day we have the chance to celebrate the love You have bestowed upon us. Let us do so with every part of our hearts and souls. Bless our sacred union, Lord.

Essential NINE:

Endure

Love…endures all things.

1 Corinthians 13:4,7

Endure

Endurance is more than perseverance. I think one of the best descriptions of endurance is found in 1 Corinthians 13:7: "[Love] bears all things, believes all things, hopes all things, endures all things." Endurance requires bearing up and continuing for prolonged times under adverse circumstances.

The old adage "There is no substitute for time" is especially true when it comes to marriage. There are things that must be worked through with prayer, God's Word, and simple perseverance. I have seen time work amazing things into our marriage. It has a way of turning every struggle into a victory, every difficulty into a bonding experience, and every misunderstanding into deeper understanding. But all this takes a period of time and not just a moment or a day.

It also takes ongoing intention and perseverance and not just a thought, a passing notion, or yet another resolution. Marriage is a growing entity. Nurture it and stand firmly on God's foundation of strength and grace so you can see beyond this moment to a loving, fulfilling, and lasting relationship.

Shaping a Godly Marriage

Beforehand, everyone has a somewhat fantastical idea of what marriage with the one they make their vows to will be like, but the reality can be a stark contrast to what was imagined. Brian and I definitely had different ideas of what we thought our relationship would look like. We never imagined financial difficulties, teenagers, misunderstandings, or illness would be a part of our happily-ever-after. In fact, while we were in premarital counseling I was certain that the majority of the advice we got was simply unnecessary. The pastor clearly didn't know what a perfectly godly and compatible couple he was dealing with and what a perfect picture of a godly marriage we would become. Was I in for a wake-up call!

I didn't realize how much effort, care, prayer, learning, growing, and paying attention would be invested over the long term before the full picture of a godly marriage could be understood, let alone come into being!

Isn't it interesting how time adds flavor and value to so many things? As a little girl I used to think speed was a virtue. I could color a whole coloring book in a matter of an hour when I was five. I remember putting my multitude of completed pictures up against the work of a little girl who had spent her whole time painstakingly coloring in one scene. We compared our pictures. Not once had she colored over a line. She had used a variety of different colors, matching every tone with each other. Her picture was beautiful. Mine was a mess of scribbles that never considered lines or varieties of color. She had taken her time, and I had rushed through the coloring book.

Endurance is the value time bestows on marriage. Endurance showcases the strength, grace, and value of marriage. It is the quality that allows you to hang on to the relationship and go and grow through the hard times together. Endurance would not have value if it did not win its marks through hard times. It is the weathering of circumstances and the triumphing through the trials that give marriage its greatest worth.

Altar Promises

B As we stood at the altar and repeated the vows that millions upon millions of couples over the years have taken, I didn't realize how many opportunities there would be to fulfill them. Actually, I don't know that I even paid that much attention to their precise meaning, being more concerned to make sure I said them properly. One of the crazy fears I had as a kid was that I would never be able to get married because I wouldn't be able to remember the words I was supposed to repeat at the altar. So there I was, intensely focusing on saying the right words but missing what the words really meant.

I think that is a common occurrence even for those without the fears that I had. Do you remember the words to those vows? They go like this:

> I, _____, take thee, _____, as my lawfully wedded (wife or husband), to have and to hold from this day forward, for better or for worse, for rich or for poor, in sickness and in health, to love and to cherish, until death do us part. And according to God's holy ordinance, I pledge you my love.

In making those vows, we were making a lifetime commitment to one another, through thick and thin. I don't know exactly who came up with those vows, but I can tell you from experience they had a very realistic view of married life.

In Sickness and in Health

When Cheryl and I got married I'd never had a sick day in my life—well, maybe one or two here and there, but you know what I mean. Back in those days I was still surfing three or four days a week and had spent the previous three years as an amateur boxer. The point being this—I was in really good shape. Little did we know that everything would soon change.

About two-and-a-half years into our marriage I began to feel rundown and extremely fatigued. Day after day I seemed to be getting weaker and weaker, until one day I came home from work and collapsed. After that day I did not get out of bed again for more than three months. There I was, this once strong and perfectly fit 26-year-old, having to be helped to the bathroom, and hardly capable of even bringing my food from my plate to my mouth. The fatigue was so severe that I thought I was dying of some yet undiagnosed disease. This was the beginning of life with a chronic illness, and there at my side was my young bride, pregnant and shortly due to deliver our second child.

In the early 1980s no one knew what this strange syndrome was, though it would eventually affect hundreds of thousands of people around the world. Today there is a name for it and a diagnosis. It is called Epstein-Barr virus; chronic fatigue syndrome (CFS); or as it is known in Britain, ME (myalgic encephalomyelitis). This debilitating illness has come and gone with varying degrees of intensity throughout these 27 years of our lives, right up to the present day. And through it all Cheryl has faithfully nursed me through the ups and downs.

This is what "for better or for worse" and in "sickness and in health" has meant. It has not been easy for her. There have been many times when I was unable to fulfill my basic duties as a husband, father, provider, and so on, but she has never once complained or expressed disappointment at the way our lives have gone. Quite the opposite in fact—she has always been right there to encourage me to trust the Lord; to make the necessary adjustments in the way we live that would contribute to my general recovery, and to go the extra mile in attending to my needs in every way possible to help me deal with this thing that could have easily ripped our young marriage apart. By God's grace the condition has been much milder over the past several years and we live pretty normal lives. Yet a special part of our lives today is having endured through those difficult years.

Looking back, I don't know that I would change anything. Sure, I would like to have felt better. And without CFS, no doubt things would have been much easier on our family. But there's something so deep and profound Cheryl and I share today because of those times of suffering together, and I wouldn't trade it for anything.

There's a verse in Paul's second letter to Timothy that says, "If we endure, we shall also reign with Him." That same truth applies in the marriage relationship. If we endure, if we persevere through the difficult and challenging times, we will reign. In other words, all of the hard times are laying a foundation for a fruitful, joyful, meaningful, even blissful future. That's where we've come to after 30 years of marriage.

We are experiencing our best years together and enjoying one another more than we ever imagined we could.

Till Death Do Us Part

Cheryl referred to the scripture that tells us that love "endures all things." The verse that comes to my mind regarding endurance is, "Let us run with endurance the race that is set before us" (Hebrews 12:1). Endurance means being able to go the distance, to keep moving forward despite the opposition or regardless of the seeming slowness of the pace.

There are difficult times in every marriage where it seems like you're getting nowhere, where it looks like things are never going to change, never going to improve—and this is when endurance is needed. Sometimes after everything else has been said in marital counseling, the last word is simply "Hang in there."

Most people don't want to hear that. They want everything to change immediately, but it just doesn't happen that way. Important things in life take time. We hear about certain things that are better because of age. Wine, cheese, beef are all better if they've gone through an aging process, the passing of time. We refer to people who are wise or knowledgeable as "seasoned," meaning they've been around; they know what they know because they've lived through the ups and downs. They've endured, and they've come through as better people.

Endurance builds character according to Paul in Romans 5:3-4, and that is exactly why God allows us to go through challenging times. He's seeking to develop our character, and that's true for married couples too.

Have you ever witnessed the wonder of a loving, godly couple whose character has been forged by the trials of life and the grace of God? They seem solid, kind, generous, and connected. They are often the couple others seek out for advice, solace, and wisdom.

This is the kind of couple God wants you and your spouse to be. Not shallow, superficial pretenders, but deep, genuine, real people He can set forth as examples of what He intended marriage to be. Again, to endure means to stick with it all the way to the end, to go the distance...and the distance in this case is "till death do us part."

A Woman's Obstacles to Endurance

C What are the things that assault marriage and threaten the quality of endurance? There are financial difficulties, internal struggles with children, outside influences, emotional issues, illness, and misunderstandings. These things can either strengthen the marriage or be the cause of its dissolution. Often the factor that gives these issues power is a woman's need for security. Women crave security emotionally, relationally, physically, and financially. When it is threatened a woman will often begin to look outside of her marriage for that security she craves.

There seems to be an increase in the number of women who quit too early and too easily on marriage. I will never forget talking to a young woman who had given up after only a few years. She and her husband were struggling financially and she was looking for a quick fix to her financial woes. She found it in another man, who was wealthy. She filed for divorce and remarried soon after.

About a year into her new marriage, she called me. She was woeful. Her first husband had made a financial recovery and was involved in a new relationship. My friend spent an hour explaining to me how she could have saved that marriage with a little effort. She was upset that her ex-husband was moving on. Though she treasured the financial security in this new relationship, she still had feelings for her first husband. What a mess!

This woman gave up on a great marriage and walked away from a wonderful man because her need for financial security overwhelmed her. Later she rued that fateful action.

Emotional Insecurities

When a woman feels emotionally insecure she will sometimes seek that emotional security in another relationship. She will become extremely close to her girlfriends or even seek out a new love interest. Through the use of the Internet, many women, insecure because of their age and fading beauty, have been pursuing new relationships. Lately, I have been talking to a lot of women who have dabbled in some very dangerous communications via their home computer. Almost every excuse offered begins with, "Well, I wasn't feeling that desirable anymore…" or "I just wanted to see if I could still attract someone else."

This is dangerous territory for any woman, let alone a married one. Some of these women have been married over 20 years and have grown children. Their emotional insecurities are so strong that they lose sight of the value of the relationship they already have with the man who has come home faithfully every night for more than two decades.

Desire for Protection

Women want to feel cherished, adored, and taken care of. Don't we all want to feel physically protected? With our husband's arm around our shoulders, we feel the comfort of his presence but also a sense of physical safety. But that gesture and the sentiment and security behind it might fade from our routine after a few years of marriage.

When a woman feels like her husband has lost that protective, caring nature, she will often seek out the attention of another man. If a gentleman opens the door for her or offers to fix her car or provide for her in any way, there comes that moment when she might resort to dangerous thoughts: "My husband doesn't love and protect me anymore! He doesn't look out for me. He doesn't care about me like this man does."

Many couples don't even hold hands after a certain point in marriage. Women don't perceive holding hands as just a gesture of affection. They really do attach a sense of physical security to such simple actions. And such actions are easy habits to restore to a marriage.

Misunderstandings and Fantasies

Misunderstandings can make a woman feel extremely insecure. As women, we tend to jump to all sorts of irrational conclusions when we are misunderstood. I have a bad habit of taking every issue Brian and I face to another level. He's talking about one thing but I will assume he is really saying he doesn't like something about me. The way my mind works can often be very convoluted and confusing. And bottom line, this way of distorting conversations and information is the way of deception, not truth.

A man can move on from a misunderstanding in a noninvolved manner, convinced that it will work itself out with time. Not so for a woman! We take issue with wording and phrases and want to know what they meant by every statement they made. A misunderstanding is reason to look for the security of being understood. We are afraid that if we are not understood we will be neglected or, worse yet, rejected.

Women's insecurities are a big target area of the enemy. Think back to the Garden of Eden—in Genesis 3 you will find Satan playing on Eve's insecurities. His subtle suggestions made her feel insecure about her fulfillment, intelligence, and knowledge. Has anything really changed since then?

Even when they're aware of this, when the daily routine seems too "normal" to bear yet again, women want to test the waters with strangers. Men are prone to the same desires. The what-if factor is very tempting. But there are so many risks to one's heart and one's life when a person pursues a connection with someone they have never met. Many wives are destroying their integrity and their heart connections with their spouses because they think that a bit of anonymous flirting or a few playful exchanges via e-mail or texting are "safe." Don't fall prey to this thinking.

Endurance requires recognizing insecurity as insecurity and then submitting that same insecurity to God. He is able to do amazing things with deficits, difficulties, and debt! And ironically, endurance brings the security to marriage that women crave.

A Man's Obstacles to Endurance

B The threats to endurance for men are different than they are for women. If I had to pinpoint one thing that hinders men from going the distance in their marriages it would have to be immaturity—both practical and spiritual immaturity.

Practical immaturity manifests itself in an unwillingness to grow up and face the fact that married life is not all fun and games. Some guys refuse to grow up and seem to want to remain teenagers forever. They want their wives to be a forever girlfriend instead of a wife and partner who is also maturing. They want someone who meets their needs but doesn't require anything in return. One who is there to cook and clean and have sex and take care of the kids, but not one who says, "I need your help, your attention, your time, your partnership."

Some guys, though perhaps mature in the practical sense, suffer from *spiritual immaturity* and do not have a deep commitment to Christ. They've never thought to deny themselves, take up their crosses, and follow Jesus. They've never taken seriously the command for husbands to love their wives as Christ loved the church. Their spiritual life is more about financial and material prosperity than about living for the glory of God whatever the cost.

Men, unless we make a conscious choice to grow up and become men of God we'll never endure. But we don't really have that choice now. We've made a commitment, and God expects us to be faithful to that commitment. The good news is, He'll give us all we need to ensure that we endure to the end.

Endurance Brings Perspective

Robert Browning, the poet, is often quoted for these famous lines: "Grow old along with me! The best is yet to be, the last of life, for which the first was made: Our times are in His hand." As a young wife, I didn't understand the glory of such words. Now, as I pass middle age, I understand the depth and delight of this poetry. The best times of marriage were not in the beginning. Those years were the seedlings sown for the rich harvest we now enjoy. You also can discover this great blessing of wisdom and preparation for the best as you grow together as husband and wife.

Brian and I were kids when we got married. As he attested to earlier, he was more concerned about saying the wedding vows correctly than what he was pledging to. In the same way, I was so entranced by the wedding that I hardly took notice of what I was promising to do for the rest of my earthly life. It was those silly youths who were forced to grow up together through financial struggles, emotional upheavals, and hard circumstances and who became the adults we are today. But we aren't through growing! Both of us are always exploring new challenges and learning new and deeper lessons in the Word of God.

Recently, we spoke with a couple who had almost lost hope for their marriage. They were holding on by a thread. As we listened to their struggles, Brian and I were unable to suppress our laughter. The couple looked at us in surprise, perhaps a bit offended.

"Don't you see the wonderful comic element in your relationship?" I asked.

Their eyes widened. "Don't take yourselves too seriously," I continued. "These are the places you are growing out of. It is these very things you will look back on and laugh at in years to come."

Soon this young couple was laughing with us at some of their escapades. Laughter and humor make up one of the greatest rewards of endurance.

The Joy of the Journey

B As we've both said, we were young, immature, and naïve when we got married, but God has been faithful to keep us through all the ups and downs. And here we are reaping the blessings of having sown to the Spirit all these years.

I'm not saying we've always done everything right or that we haven't sinned or done plenty of stupid things over the years. What I am saying is that in the "big picture" we've continued to put Jesus first in our lives, trusting and obeying Him, and He has blessed us.

If I chose one word to describe our lives today it would be *joyful*. There's joy in walking and talking and laughing together. There's joy in spending time with our children and grandchildren. There's joy in friendships we've shared together over the years. There's joy in growing old together and falling more in love as the years pass. There's joy in serving Jesus together in new and exciting ways. There's joy in watching each other being fashioned more and more into the image of Jesus Christ our Lord. Endurance has its payday. The Scriptures say of Jesus that for the joy set before Him, He endured the cross.

As you endure, as you persevere, as you stick with it and are faithful…as you hang in there, trusting the Lord…remember this: Those who sow in tears will reap in joy.

The Rewards of Endurance

Endurance is the transforming element in marriage. You might marry when you still feel like a kid, but time, trials, and tests mixed with grace turn us into adults. At no set point can you turn to your spouse and say, "You are now what you will always be." Spouses, like marriages, are always growing in grace and maturity. This is one of the wondrous rewards of the marital union.

Security, laughter, and transformation are not the only rewards of endurance though. Endurance also brings mutual respect and appreciation. We are still discovering the richness of one another's character after 30 years of marriage. And of course, marriage and faith and endurance are making our individual characters more godly each and every day. What a gift it is to watch the person you love become more and more the person God created them to be!

A strong marriage, an enduring marriage, is a great legacy for your children. When they see the quality of perseverance in their parents' relationship, they understand that they also can persevere through the trials and tests of life. They quickly perceive how kindness, compassion, and grace are healthy responses that allow husbands, wives, and families to move past misunderstandings, disagreements, and character flaws.

We have endured simply by holding on to our marriage and seeking the Lord, asking Him to come and work in every trial and in every opportunity. This, friends, is what you can do as well. Hold hands, hold one another up in prayer, and hold on to your marriage with every part of your being.

KNOWING IS GROWING

1. What were your mutual misconceptions when you first married? Talk about whether you felt that you knew it all or knew nothing about marriage.

2. As you look back on the advice and counsel you received before marriage with the hindsight wisdom that you have now, what do you wish you had known? What do you both have to share with a newlywed couple about the significance and the blessing of the marriage vows?

3. What trials have come your way during your marriage that have strengthened, renewed, and enhanced your relationship? Explore how God has provided what you need at the right times. How has the word *endurance* taken on meaning of blessing rather than hardship?

4. What are obstacles to endurance, both individually and together? Pray for one another in these specific areas of need. And give your marriage to God daily so every trial and triumph becomes a stepping-stone along your path of enduring love.

5. List your areas of joy, and laugh about your learning curves over the years. Then look at one another and express your sincere gratitude for each other's willingness to endure, persevere, and press on in the joys of marriage. List specific ways in which your spouse delights you and has honored their vows over the years in special ways.

GROWING-TOGETHER GRACE

Dear Lord, You are so good to us. How many times have we encountered obstacles or created those barriers to a godly marriage, and You have provided a way for us to continue? Prepare our minds to be in line with Your will and Your way. Prepare our hearts so that we protect them from outside influence or temptation, Lord. Give us like minds and dreams so we partner together toward our future.

God, please bless our union and remind us of the many joys and achievements we have savored along the way. We praise You for the creation of marriage. We are deeply grateful for the vows we took before You and because of You in order to begin our journey together as husband and wife.

E.Y.E.:
Examine Yourself Essential

*Let each one examine his own work, and then he will
have rejoicing in himself alone, and not in another.*

Galatians 6:4

Examine Yourself Essential

It began as so many of their arguments had. They were in the car alone. It was meant to be a date night, a reprieve from the responsibilities of managing a growing household. On their way to a romantic dinner, the husband rather casually suggested improvements to his wife's parenting. "I think you need to go a little easier on Seth," he started. He was never able to finish the thought.

Suddenly, like a volcanic eruption, the emotions the wife had been holding on to for years burst forth. Her many resentments flowed out: She felt as if she were raising their children alone. The husband was always busy with work or clients. He often missed dinners with the family and rarely had time to tuck the kids into bed. She was the one who helped them with their homework, assigned tasks, enforced good behavior, settled disputes, and listened to their heartaches. She knew everything that was going on in the lives of her children—and now Mr. Never-Emotionally-There was giving her tips on how to mother! Well, she had a few suggestions for him too!

Can you imagine this scene? Have you lived out something similar? You can probably envision what took place next…

They never made it to dinner. The anger in the car was so hot that she opened the door at the first red light and walked home. He drove aimlessly for hours, finally grabbing a burger at a 24-hour drive-thru before returning home late that evening. She was already in bed, feigning sleep. Neither spouse was ready to receive or give an apology.

The stalemate continued for days until a truce ensued. Civilities revived, but the deep resentment loomed very close to the surface in both spouses.

That story is so typical of many of the marital disagreements we hear about. It seems they all begin with "helpful suggestions" for the other spouse's "improvement." The improvements can be anything: spiritual, emotional, physical.

The wife might suggest the husband remove fat from his diet. This suggestion might be met with a countersuggestion from the husband that his wife not nag so much. You can imagine the suggestions that follow. Or perhaps you've experienced this exact conversation firsthand.

"Helpful Suggestions," to give it a name, is an age-old argument that started almost at the beginning of creation. Soon after the very first married couple disobeyed God about partaking of the forbidden fruit, the blame game or "helpful suggestions with ulterior motives" began. Call it part of the curse, if you will.

When God asked Adam if he had eaten of the forbidden tree, he answered, "The woman whom You gave to be with me, she gave me of the tree, and I ate" (Genesis 3:12). In other words, "It was You who gave me this woman, and if she had acted as she was supposed to, I wouldn't have acted as I did. It's her fault."

That's the way it goes in arguments. The husband refuses to love his wife until she submits. In the same ugly spirit, the wife refuses to submit to the husband until he starts loving her as Christ loved the church. This type of argument will probably be ongoing because each spouse refuses to change until the other acts first. And the root of the argument comes from wounds within each partner. Neither feels loved or supported.

In Galatians 6:4-5, the apostle Paul said,

> Let each one examine his own work, and then he will have
> rejoicing in himself alone, and not in another. For each one
> shall bear his own load.

When we focus on what our marriage partner should be doing, we lose sight of what *we* should be doing. When we focus only on what is missing from the relationship, then we miss the chance to examine how our own actions and behaviors can help repair or improve the situation. Not only does our marriage flag, but our walk with the Lord is also affected. We stop growing spiritually because we are waiting for our spouse to dramatically improve spiritually before we obey God's directives to us.

God has given directives to each man that he is to do regardless of his wife's attitude or actions. The husband answers to God. In the same manner, the wife has been given biblical directives that she is to follow "as unto the Lord," not as unto her husband.

"Helpful Improvements"

C Let's face it, women love fixer-uppers. When they see a house in need of some TLC they know their touch is needed, and they are ready and eager to offer it. The nurturing aspect of a woman blossoms, and she feels fulfilled as she adds her beauty, creativity, and talent to the shabby structure, making it a thing of beauty in the process.

In a similar fashion, a woman often likes to see the man she marries as a project to which she can make improvements. She likes to style his hair, choose his clothes, improve his health, brighten his outlook on life, and even help him change or build on his occupation. In so doing, she feels she is actually helping her husband become his best. This whole process also becomes her way, directly or indirectly, of showcasing her flair for improving any project she is given.

A man often resents these changes. Rather than feeling enhanced he feels belittled, disrespected, and unaccepted—that his wife is trying to control him. He resists every effort the wife enlists for his betterment. In turn, this often makes the wife resentful and angry. She was only trying to help him, right?

But what about the men? Men have this wonderful way of wanting to dominate. They are always conforming things into their own image. They rarely acknowledge their wife's fears or reservations—instead, a husband will tell his wife to simply be brave or to do it herself. Phrases like, "Quit acting that way"; "Why do you always do that?"; and "Don't do that again!" are often thrown his wife's way. A man thinks he wants his wife to feel and act like him, but would you really like to be married to yourself?

When God created man and woman, He created them to complement each other. As He contemplated the creation of woman He said, "I will make a helper comparable to him." The great purpose of "woman" was to complete the man. The man was incomplete, lacking, without her. God created her with capabilities and gifts the man was lacking. Not only was she created to complement him, but she was created to be a companion to him.

The man was already created with qualities that would complement God's new creation, woman. Together the man and woman would be a whole...the two would become one flesh. The word "one" used in Genesis 2:24 is the Hebrew word *echad*. This word has the connotation of diversity in unity. It is often referred to as a "compound unity."

The man was not created to dominate the woman, nor was the woman created to control the man. God created each to complement the other and to create a whole between the two of them. Both bring something unique that the other does not have to the marriage. This is why helpful hints really don't work.

Questions Women Shouldn't Ask and Men Shouldn't Answer...

On a side note, sometimes we invite the helpful suggestions we don't want to hear. A wife might ask her husband a question she hopes will bring self-affirmation; however, she is never really pleased with the answer. Some such questions include the following:

1. Do I look like I've gained weight?
2. Do you think I've aged?
3. Do you ever think about your old girlfriends?
4. How can I be a better wife?
5. Do you think she's pretty?

Men, these are trick questions, so don't answer them! Just smile pleasantly and tell her how much you love her.

Men make statements rather than ask questions:

1. I don't look as old as most men my age do.
2. I can pretty much eat anything I want and not
   gain weight.
3. I'm still in great shape.
4. I'm still cool.
5. I don't need to read the instructions or follow
   the directions.

Women, remember to leave these statements alone! A kind smile
is all that is needed.

Self-Examination

How do we stop the endless cycle of helpful hints? We apply ourselves to our own God-given roles. We must look at the Scriptures—
to what God specifically says to the men about how they are to behave.
Notice also that God doesn't tell the women how He wants the men
to behave. He speaks directly to the men.

He also speaks directly to the women regarding their behavior in
the marriage. He does not tell the men to enforce a certain behavior
in their wives. In a recent counseling appointment the man intimated
that he needed to remind his wife of God's directives or she wouldn't
remember to do them. I told him that prayer would be a lot more effective…and much safer too!

As the husband concentrates on obeying God in his role, rather than
on his wife's obedience to God, he will grow spiritually. As the husband
grows spiritually, he will become a greater and better influence on his
marriage. God will bless the man who obeys Him. Jesus promised in
John 14:23, "If anyone loves Me, he will keep My word; and My Father
will love him, and We will come to him and make Our home with him."

Imagine the glory of that promise! When a man loves Jesus, he
obeys Jesus' word. When He obeys Jesus' word, God the Father makes
His home in the heart and life of that man.

The same is true for the woman that chooses to obey the word of

Jesus. When a woman chooses to obey the Scripture's directives to her out of love for Jesus, the Father and the Son make their abode with her. This is a promise of blessing.

So rather than concentrating on what our partner is or is not doing, it is important that we realize we are standing before God individually for what we are doing and not doing!

A WORD TO THE MEN:

E.Y.E. Through the Lens of Scripture

B There is no better way to review, assess, and change your life than to examine it through the lens of God's Word. Prayerfully consider the following scriptures:

> *Husbands, love your wives, just as Christ also loved the church and gave Himself for her, that He might sanctify and cleanse her with the washing of water by the word, that He might present her to Himself a glorious church, not having spot or wrinkle or any such thing, but that she should be holy and without blemish.*
>
> *So husbands ought to love their own wives as their own bodies; he who loves his wife loves himself. For no one ever hated his own flesh, but nourishes and cherishes it, just as the Lord does the church. For we are members of His body, of His flesh and of His bones. "For this reason a man shall leave his father and mother and be joined to his wife, and the two shall become one flesh."*
>
> *This is a great mystery, but I speak concerning Christ and the church. Nevertheless let each one of you in particular so love his own wife as himself, and let the wife see that she respects her husband.*
>
> EPHESIANS 5:25-33

> *Husbands, love your wives and do not be bitter toward them.*
>
> COLOSSIANS 3:19

Husbands, likewise, dwell with them with understanding, giving honor to the wife, as to the weaker vessel, and as being heirs together of the grace of life, that your prayers may not be hindered.

Finally, all of you be of one mind, having compassion for one another; love as brothers, be tenderhearted, be courteous; not returning evil for evil or reviling for reviling, but on the contrary blessing, knowing that you were called to this, that you may inherit a blessing.

1 PETER 3:7-9

A WORD TO THE WOMEN:

E.Y.E. Through the Lens of Scripture

C Now, here are a few scriptures for the wives to concentrate on. Remember you are doing this for Jesus. Pray over each passage and ask God to help you to obey Him in His directives for you.

Wives, submit to your own husbands, as to the Lord. For the husband is head of the wife, as also Christ is head of the church; and He is the Savior of the body. Therefore, just as the church is subject to Christ, so let the wives be to their own husbands in everything.

EPHESIANS 5:22-24

Wives, submit to your own husbands,
as is fitting in the Lord.

COLOSSIANS 3:18

Wives, likewise be submissive to your own husbands, that even if some do not obey the word, they, without a word, may be won by the conduct of their wives, when they observe your chaste conduct accompanied by fear. Do not let your adornment be merely outward—arranging of the hair, wearing gold, or putting on fine apparel—rather let it be the hidden person of the heart, with the incorruptible beauty of a gentle and quiet spirit, which is very precious in the sight of God. For in this manner, in former times, the holy women who trusted in God also adorned themselves, being submissive to their own husbands, as Sarah obeyed Abraham, calling him lord, whose daughters you are if you do good and are not afraid with any terror.

1 PETER 3:1-6

Clearing the Way for Obedience

What keeps us from simply obeying the directives that God has for us in marriage? Many of us know what to do, but when faced with the opportunity to follow His leading and His commands, we hold back and make a less desirable choice, follow a deception, or indulge in sinful behavior. We might have regrets even as we are making the less-than-godly decision or as we clean up the mess in the aftermath of our large or small disobedience. And yet we find ourselves creating barriers between ourselves and God and His purpose for our marriage.

Recently I was doing a radio interview, and the host invited the listeners to call in and talk to me about the book I had recently written, *When a Woman Lets Go of Her Fears.* Two women I spoke to on the radio that day talked about their fear of submitting to and trusting their husbands. The first said she couldn't do either but couldn't provide a definite reason why. The second caller wanted to encourage the first woman to *not* trust her husband. She proceeded to elaborate on all the suffering that had come because she had trusted her first husband, who had let her down.

When I was finally able to get a word in, I reminded the callers that the Bible never instructs women to trust their husbands. Far from it! The Bible instructs women to trust the *Lord.* The Old Testament even states, "Cursed is the man who trusts in man" (Jeremiah 17:5). Submission is the ultimate act of trusting the Lord. The wife submits to the husband to show her trust for the Lord. By submitting, the woman is declaring that God will take care of remedying the issue or situation as she obeys the biblical command to submit.

Many women, like men, refuse to simply concentrate on obeying God's instruction to them because they fear they will be taken advantage of. The wife fears that the husband will disrespect her and she will become a doormat. The husband fears that the wife will dominate the marriage and take advantage of him.

Another fear a marriage partner can have is that the other will never change, and their personal obedience will only make the disobedient spouse feel vindicated.

Still others fear they will be the one doing all the work until one or the other dies. They fear there will never be mutual cooperation.

Fear is an act of distrust and is no excuse for disobedience. Again, we must obey God regardless of what we fear the consequences are going to be. Taking this a step further, we are to obey because by faith we choose to believe that God will bless our obedience as He has promised.

It is pride, however, that is probably the greatest obstacle to obedience. When I refuse to recognize that I need self-examination in the light of Scripture I am prideful.

Pride is also at the base of the blame-the-spouse problem. It is so much easier to believe that our spouse has the issues than to acknowledge we actually could stand some God-improvements!

I heard a speaker share how, for years, she tried to "fix" her husband. It seemed all her "helpful suggestions" for his spiritual growth were met with strong resistance. Finally she started praying in earnest for him. One day as she was praying she received a vision from the Lord.

In her mind, she saw two potter's wheels furiously turning as the Great Potter worked His beautiful design on the spinning clay. One pot was being formed on each wheel. She watched as the pot on the right wheel reached a hand over and started helping the Potter form the clay on the left wheel. *That's you,* she felt the Lord speak to her heart.

You are trying to help me form and mold your husband. I know what I am doing. Hands off!

The woman chuckled as she recalled the Lord's word to her. But what an apt description of what we are often doing in our marriages! We forget that our spouse, as well as we ourselves, is on the wheel of the Great Potter. God is forming both of us according to His design, pleasure, and purposes.

Crisis Calls for Greater Obedience

Recently a woman came to us for counseling. Her husband was involved in some shady activity. She was beside herself. However, her issue was not how she could obey God, but rather how she could help and even save her husband.

We explained to her that she couldn't help or save her husband. She could, though, help herself. We outlined how she needed to surrender more fully to God and seek to obey Him. The more she would seek Him, the greater help she would be to Him as *He* worked to save her husband.

This is true for either partner. The wife cannot save or even change her husband. Nor can the husband change or save the wife. Both the husband and the wife need to receive their biblical directives individually and seek God for the power to carry out those same directives.

The Reward of Examining Ourselves

What happens when we examine ourselves? Well, the first thing that happens is that we begin to take responsibility for our own actions. The process of taking responsibility opens us up for repentance, change, and spiritual growth.

As repentance takes place we are set free from bad attitudes, bad habits, and fears. This causes spiritual growth, which brings God's blessing into our lives and subsequently into our marriages.

The essential of self-examination cannot be ignored. So hold back on extending helpful suggestions to your spouse—instead, pray and ask God to work in you the things that are well-pleasing in His sight. Then stand back and get ready to be blessed in extraordinary ways!

Looking Forward

As we stood there at the altar, the pastor said, "Brian and Cheryl, the day has finally arrived—the day you've been praying about, the day you've been planning for, the day you've anticipated. The day when you would be standing before God and this company, taking vows of love and faithfulness, and thereby entering into the deepest, most intimate, most abiding relationship God has ordained for man, the relationship of husband and wife."

He was absolutely right! Apart from our relationship with Jesus, marriage has been the deepest, most intimate, and most abiding relationship we've ever known. It has proven to be God's good gift for our benefit and enjoyment, just as He said it was…and yes, "The best is yet to be."

As you work on each of the essentials we've covered in this journey together, take time to notice your strides of spiritual maturity and growth. Celebrate those milestones and meaningful steps toward one another and God.

Evaluate yourself in light of all of the essentials for growing together now. And we highly recommend that you do the same in six months' time. Take stock of your marriage in these categories and see how you are doing. Don't make it a test or a competition, but do take time to be aware of the health of your relationship, your faith, and your personal willingness to invest in your marriage.

Your relationship is a gift to treasure. Can you see its beauty? Do you see God's hand upon it and His love working through it? Marriage is indeed a God-thing. Savor the blessings as you draw closer emotionally, physically, mentally, and spiritually. And give God the glory as your marriage becomes a light for others. "And whatever you do, do it heartily, as to the Lord and not to men, knowing that from the Lord you will receive the reward of the inheritance; for you serve the Lord Christ" (Colossians 3:23-24).

KNOWING IS GROWING

1. When have you tried to fix each other or resolve one another's troubles? How did that go? Are you still trying to do this even now?

2. Turn the examining eye upon each of yourselves. Spend time thinking about the Scripture selections provided in this chapter. Pray as individuals and ask God to enlighten your hearts and minds so you each know what areas of growth are your responsibilities.

3. Free each other from scrutiny. Extend grace to one another. Let go of those lists of past transgressions or the flaws you wish you could fix in the other. Instead, consider what God calls you to nurture in your own spiritual maturity.

4. What an amazing journey this has been! Look back at the different ways you can grow together as a couple. Discuss which lessons stand out the most to you. What have you learned about your marriage, yourself, and God?

GROWING-TOGETHER GRACE

Creator of marriage, we come to You with great gladness and gratitude. Today we recommit ourselves to growing together as Your children and as a couple devoted to each other and to our walks of faith. Remind us of the tender mercies we have received. Forgive us for our times of unforgiveness or hurtful actions and words against one another. Unite us in heart, mind, and spirit so we continue on the path You have shaped for us with great conviction and confidence.

We love You, Lord. Fill us with the desire to love as Christ loved and to serve as Christ served. Thank You for the great privilege of growing together and for the knowledge that the best is yet to be because of Your wonderful blessing.

Essentials in
ACTION

God created man in His own image; in the image of God He created him; male and female He created them. Then God blessed them.

GENESIS 1:27-28

Essentials in Action

We hope you have enjoyed and benefited from this journey through the biblical essentials we've found valuable and beneficial for our marriage. We feel privileged to have accompanied you as we've shared our story. We hope that, through our telling you the ups and downs and the times of great growth we've experienced, you have found encouragement and insight for your own marriage.

As we bring this book to a close, we want to exhort you to put these principles we've shared into practice. The word *exhort* means "to strongly encourage or urge (someone) to do something." As we've said, we've been married and in the ministry for quite some time. As a result we have seen God do many amazing things, not only in our lives as a married couple, but in the lives of many others as well.

We want to encourage you with some of the amazing things we've seen the Lord do over the years. We have seen marriages that barely resembled marriages be turned "right side up" by the power of the Holy Spirit. We've seen couples who had gone so far as to divorce have their marriages restored and made better than ever. We have seen newly-wed couples who thought their marriage was a mistake come under the instruction of the Word, settle into their relationship, and experience wonderful blessings.

As has been said before, you don't pick a good or a bad marriage off the shelf; marriage is what you make it. By the grace God gives us, we can all do it right and enjoy the blessings if we grasp onto the essentials He has given us.

God's Word Is the First Word

Many of us scramble to find our own way through life and marriage, and it takes extreme weariness or trials to wake us up to God's way. I'll never forget the first time I had the opportunity to do some marriage counseling, I was 24 years old and about as green as anyone could be. (For you younger readers, "green" refers to being inexperienced, not to being an environmentalist.) So there I was waiting for my very first couple to come in for marriage counseling…and when they arrived I almost fell off my chair. They were in their eighties and had been married for over 60 years! I'd been married for less than a year and in the ministry for even less than that.

What did I do? I listened to them as they opened up about their problems. I knew that my own life wisdom wasn't going to compare to theirs, so I avoided offering that and went to God's Word. I shared a few Bible verses I had been meditating on and was being blessed by in my own life. Then I prayed for them and sent them on their way. I was absolutely amazed when I got a letter from them a few weeks later telling me how much our time together had helped them with their issues.

Thankfully, both Cheryl and I learned early on the power of the Word of God when it is believed and applied to marriage. Recently, we were asked to speak at a couple's retreat. As we shared on Saturday morning during the first session I was feeling really dull and uninspired. Afterward Cheryl asked me what was wrong and why I was so unenthusiastic and boring. I knew she was right about my presentation, but I couldn't seem to pull it together. (This is not how you want to feel at a speaking engagement!)

Well, nothing really changed during the next session, except my lack of enthusiasm rubbed off on Cheryl a bit. When it was all said and done and we were driving back home, we both agreed that, at least from our point of view, the whole thing had been a flop. We joked a bit and prayed that the Lord would take our feeble effort and do something with it.

I was completely astounded the following week when one of the students in my Bible college class came and thanked me for being instrumental in saving his parents' marriage. He proceeded to tell me that they had been at the retreat that weekend in a last-ditch effort to keep their relationship together. The things Cheryl and I shared had really touched their hearts, he said, and had led them to make a fresh commitment to the Lord and one another. Wow! Once again we had the privilege of seeing firsthand the power of God's Word working in people's lives.

Growing Truly Is Knowing

The other day Cheryl and I were talking to a young couple who is going through some turbulence in their marriage. They were asking how they could attain the serenity they saw in our lives as a couple. Cheryl and I both chuckled. We shared with them that things haven't always been smooth sailing, but that God is faithful. We encouraged them that as they continued to apply God's Word to their lives things would calm down and smooth out.

Their comment about the serenity in our marriage brought back to our minds a time some years ago. A dear friend of ours was sharing with us about some of the struggles he and his new bride were having in getting along with each other. As we talked to him, he said he had always admired the relationship of another couple we both knew because they were so tender, loving, and patient with each other. Then he remarked, "I had hoped to have a marriage like theirs, but I'm afraid I've got one like yours!" Cheryl and I burst out laughing, knowing he was only partially joking. There was certainly some truth to what he had said.

As we've mentioned many times over, both of us can be fiery and passionate at times. The first 15 years of our marriage that side of our personalities showed itself much more often than it does today. The funny thing is, today many people wouldn't believe we could have ever been like that. We bring this up only to underscore the reality that God is faithful. As we apply His Word to our lives, He changes us, making us more like Jesus and better suited to each other.

God desires to bless marriage. Jesus promised that He came to "give life and that more abundantly." This holds true for the marital union. God wants to make your marriage an abundant marriage.

Real Essentials for a Real Marriage

We mentioned briefly in the introduction that when we lived in England, Cheryl received a phone call asking her to do a workshop on marriage. This was for a retreat created for pastors' wives. We were still in the adjustment years, and we'd added some stress to those years by moving our family of six to England. We weren't exactly the picture-perfect couple and family during the chaos and stress of transition!

Cheryl asked the woman on the phone, "Have you heard about my marriage?" The woman countered by asking why that would make a difference. "Well, we've had some pretty lively disagreements," Cheryl told her. The woman's response was enough to convince Cheryl to speak. She was ecstatic as she exclaimed, "Praise the Lord—a real marriage!"

With this wonderful permission and encouragement to be "real" in her time of sharing with these women, Cheryl prepared her message. As we mentioned, God placed on her heart the idea of a few essentials for a healthy marriage that began with the letter "E." Cheryl's talk was transcribed, and she and I have since added to the list of essentials as we've turned to God's Word and gleaned His truths for growing a "real marriage."

About a year after Cheryl spoke, a pastor whose wife had been at the workshop shared a story about those essentials. He and his wife had not been getting along. The chasm between them was widening. When his wife returned from the retreat, he started to express, in a few choice words, all the things he thought were wrong with their union. Apparently, while his wife had been going to God and His Word, my pastor friend had been stewing and spiraling downward in his complaints and frustrations.

Well, after he vented his unhelpful gripes, his wife walked into the other room, grabbed the transcription of Cheryl's message, and threw it on the table in front of him. He might have resisted reading it out of pure stubbornness, but because he was curious about what *my wife* had to say about marriage, he picked up the pages and read them. And he confessed this to me later: He was convicted by *each* essential he read. When his wife walked back into the room, he apologized. They resolved together to incorporate godly essentials into their marriage. It has become a model for the parishioners in their church.

Isn't it a relief to know that others aren't perfect? That you and your spouse aren't the only ones who have struggles, arguments, and quirks that annoy? That you have shared jokes nobody else would get? Thank God that we receive the perfect love and grace of Christ and are given His way and Word as our light.

Essentials in Practice

Each essential we give in this book is something that has enhanced our own marriage. (They are road-tested.) And whether we are counseling a couple, talking to friends, or speaking at a marriage conference, we have found that these essentials are the very things that women and men need to incorporate into their relationships.

We also have witnessed these same essentials—entrusting, eliminating, esteeming, encouraging, exemplifying, empathizing, enlightening, energizing, and enduring—work dynamically in the lives of those we share them with, and we'd like to give you a few examples.

As is often the case, a couple had not yet recognized or addressed the spiritual element in the quarrels they'd been having. Every Saturday night they would have a huge argument that would leave them both feeling unheard, isolated, and rejected. By Sunday morning, they were too angry with one another to even consider going to church. This happened over and over, and still they weren't aware of the spiritual sabotage.

When the wife shared with Cheryl about her marital struggles, Cheryl explained the essential of enlightening her marriage and recognizing the spiritual element in conflict. So the woman went into a new week with this awareness and began to take precautions against the Saturday-night fights with her husband. Things changed drastically. Both she and her husband started to laugh when they recognized the all-too-familiar sense of building tension as the next Saturday progressed. They laughed because they understood what it was about. They knew it was spiritual, and instead of being divided on Sunday morning, they felt they were partners. The wife later said, "It wasn't that the issues stopped happening. It was more like we recognized *why* those things were happening and stopped blaming each other."

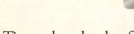

Lisa and Tim took each other for granted. They had never thought about esteeming their marriage or encouraging each other. When Lisa realized that her marriage was precious and a gift from God, her relationship to Tim took an upward turn. They began to appreciate each other and work together as a team. They even started a Bible study in their home that later became a church.

Since they first became husband and wife, Darla had been trying to change her husband. After many years of frustration, she finally learned the secret of entrusting him and her marriage to God. Though she cannot boast of a struggle-free marriage, Darla has survived the ravages of quite a few trials. In the midst of all the hardships, she has found peace in simply entrusting both her marriage and her husband to the Lord. "I gave him to God," she testifies. "Now he's God's problem. I don't have to change him, I just have to give him to God."

The chapter on examining yourself was birthed through a conversation with a young pastor. He suggested that we write a chapter called "Examining Your Mate." Both Cheryl and I felt uneasy about that whole concept. We talked about it for a long time, trying to understand where our uneasiness came from. The more we talked, the more we realized it was *self-examination* that was needed, rather than examination of the other.

We can honestly say that only when we examined ourselves and our marriage were we able to begin the journey of gathering more of God's wisdom, truths, promises, and principles to share with you. E.Y.E.—the "Examine Yourself Essential"—will become one of the most important for you and your spouse to put into practice as your marriage matures, as life brings changes, and as trials and milestones approach. Being honest and real allows you to come before God and your spouse with vulnerability, knowing that they want the best for you. That's when your heart can grow closer to God's and you and your spouse can grow closer together in godly love.

God Bless Your Marriage

It was God who in the beginning said it was not good for man to be alone. It was God who created Eve as a companion and helpmate to complete Adam. It was God who presented Eve to Adam. It was God who blessed the first marriage. Marriage is His creation and His workmanship. He wrote the handbook on how to grow together in marital faith, love, and commitment.

God means marriage, and specifically your own union, to be fulfilling, blessed, joyful, and enjoyable. We pray that you will be able to take the essentials we've discussed and apply them to your relationship in order that you might meet His highest aim for marriage. May your marriage be blessed by Him and be a blessing to others.

The rib which the LORD God had taken from
man He made into a woman, and He brought
her to the man. And Adam said:

"This is now bone of my bones
And flesh of my flesh;
She shall be called Woman,
Because she was taken out of Man."

Therefore a man shall leave his father and mother and
be joined to his wife, and they shall become one flesh.

GENESIS 2:22-24

About the Authors

Brian and Cheryl Brodersen serve together at Calvary Chapel Costa Mesa (California) and have been happily married for over 30 years. Together they have established churches, ministered to congregations, and raised their four children. One of their greatest delights is enjoying their adult children and their four grandsons. Cheryl is the daughter of well-known pastor Chuck Smith and Kay Smith; she has authored *When a Woman Lets Go of Her Fears* and co-authored *Growing Together As a Couple* with Brian. The Brodersens are popular speakers and teachers and are eager to encourage couples to embrace God's leading in their lives.

For more information about Brian and Cheryl and their ministries, please go to:

www.backtobasicsradio.com

or

www.graciouswords.com

or call:

1-800-733-6443

or write:

Brian and Cheryl Brodersen
PO Box 8000
Costa Mesa, CA 92628

Also by Cheryl Brodersen

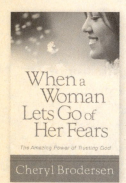

When a Woman Lets Go of Her Fears
The Amazing Power of Trusting God
CHERYL BRODERSEN

Fear in a woman's life can be controlling, deceptive, and downright crippling. You want to be free but just can't see how it can happen.

But there's help. Cheryl Brodersen, gifted speaker, author, and teacher, knows debilitating anxiety firsthand. She shares her story candidly—revealing her fears, the struggle to escape them, and how she finally broke the chains fear had wrapped around her heart and mind. As she shares practical insights, you'll discover how to...

- let go of fear's familiarity and trust God

- eliminate the "what if" fears

- use the faith you already have to fight fear

Like Cheryl, you can begin to listen to God through His Word even in the midst of your pain. You can take the first steps on a beautiful journey toward freedom...finding confidence in God and the peace that comes from leaving fear behind.

More Harvest House Resources for Your Marriage

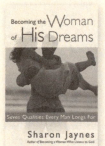

Becoming the Woman of His Dreams
Seven Qualities Every Man Longs For
SHARON JAYNES

Do you want to become the woman of your husband's dreams? The woman who makes him sorry to leave in the morning and eager to come home at night? If you would like a little "wow!" back in your relationship with the man you married, *Becoming the Woman of His Dreams* offers you an insightful look at the wonderful, unique, and God-ordained role only you have in your husband's life.

What a Wife Needs from Her Husband
Physically • Emotionally • Spiritually
MELANIE CHITWOOD

In business, finance, and sports, you need good information to make smart decisions and stay on top of your game. The same is true at home. The biblical insights and practical suggestions in this "insider's perspective" will help you step up to the next level of leadership in your home as you...

- learn more about your wife's physical and emotional needs

- replace your own unhealthy attitudes with more realistic and helpful ways of thinking

- practice not only listening to her words but also hearing her heart

The more clearly you understand exactly what your wife needs from your marriage, the more effectively you can connect with her and enjoy the fun and loving relationship God intended for you.

Is That All He Thinks About?
How to Enjoy Great Sex with Your Husband
MARLA TAVIANO

"All he wants is sex, sex, sex!"

If it seems like you and your husband are operating on different wavelengths, there's a good reason for it. God designed the differences between you and your husband to draw you together, points out Marla Taviano. So there's a lot you can do to make sex work *for* your relationship. With that positive in mind, Marla helps you to...

- stop the "meet my needs; then I'll meet yours" mind-set

- expect your husband to act like a man, not like a woman

- celebrate God's plan for you, as a woman, to be godly *and* sexual

- find forgiveness for a wrong sexual past

- discover fun, creative ideas...and a future filled with the pleasure, joy, and closeness you've always hoped for

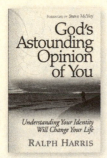

God's Astounding Opinion of You
Understanding Your Identity Will Change Your Life
RALPH HARRIS

Do you know that God's view of you is much greater than your own? Ralph Harris, founder and President of LifeCourse Ministries, leads you to embrace the Scriptures' truth about what God thinks of you—that you are special to Him, blameless, pure, and lovable.

With clear and simple explanations and examples, this resource will help you turn toward the love affair with God you were created for…a relationship in which you

- exchange fear and obligation for delight and devotion

- recognize the remarkable role and strength of the Holy Spirit in your daily life

- view your status as a *new creation* as the "new normal"— and live accordingly!

"Reading this book will change the way you think about yourself, God, the Christian life, and maybe a few other things along the way!"

DAVID GREGORY
AUTHOR OF THE BESTSELLING
DINNER WITH A PERFECT STRANGER

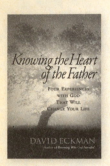

Knowing the Heart of the Father
Four Experiences with God That Will Change Your Life
DAVID ECKMAN

Perhaps Christianity seems irrelevant to where your heart is really at. Maybe you're thirsting for a *felt experience* of the Bible's truth. What if you could...

1. have an all-encompassing sense that you have a loving heavenly Dad?

2. have a sense of being enjoyed and delighted in by Him?

3. recognize that He sees you differently than you see yourself?

4. realize that *who you are* is more important to Him than *what you do?*

Do you want things to be different? See how these four great heart/soul transformations result in a vibrant, living faith that can stand up to the tests of life.